REPENTANCE

REPENTANCE

JOHN COLQUHOUN

For godly sorrow worketh repentance to salvation not to be repented of: but the sorrow of the world worketh death.

2 Corinthians 7:10

THE BANNER OF TRUTH TRUST

THE BANNER OF TRUTH TRUST
3 Murrayfield Road, Edinburgh, EH12 6EL, UK
P.O. Box 621, Carlisle, PA 17013, USA

First published 1826
First Banner of Truth Edition 1965
Reset Edition 2010

ISBN: 978 1 84871 055 9

Typeset in 10.5/14 pt Sabon Oldstyle Figures at
The Banner of Truth Trust, Edinburgh

Printed in the USA by
Versa Press, Inc.
East Peoria, IL

CONTENTS

EPITAPH ON
JOHN COLQUHOUN'S GRAVESTONE

Having studied deeply the Doctrines of
Grace, and experienced their saving
and sanctifying power in his own soul,
He laboured earnestly and affectionately
to communicate the knowledge of them
to his Fellow Sinners.
As an Author his chief aim was to advance
the Glory of the Saviour.
In private he exhibited the effects of the
holy Doctrines he inculcated in public by
a close walk with God;
And by a kind, affable and humble deportment
towards all men.
And in these several ways his labours
were acknowledged of God,
by whom they were blessed to many.
He was faithful unto death
and
has now received the Crown of Life.

BIOGRAPHICAL INTRODUCTION

While on a walking tour through Scotland during a College vacation, Alexander Moody Stuart spent a weekend at a country inn on the road between Glasgow and Edinburgh. His interest was aroused in two lads who arrived at the inn late on the Saturday evening. After spending the night there they left early next morning and returned to the inn again that evening. He discovered that they were working lads from Glasgow who, on coming under spiritual concern, had sought for a minister that preached the gospel fully. They eventually found a preacher to their mind in Edinburgh and were determined to wait on his ministry. That preacher was Dr John Colquhoun of the New Church in South Leith. Such value did they set upon Colquhoun's preaching that they were willing to walk about a hundred miles each weekend to hear him and be back at their work at 6 o'clock on Monday morning.

These young Christians were typical of many in Scotland at the beginning of last century who had felt the power of the Word and therefore highly prized the full gospel ministry at South Leith. With much of the Church of Scotland lying under the blight of unbelieving moderatism, ministries like that of Colquhoun and his contemporaries Dr John Love of Glasgow and Dr Mac-Donald of Ferintosh were oases in the desert.

John Colquhoun was born at Luss in Dunbarton-shire on 1 January, 1748. The son of a small farmer, he received his elementary education at the local Society for the Promotion of Christian Knowledge (SPCK) school. The teacher, a Christian, not only instructed the minds of his pupils but sought to impress the truth upon their hearts. It was to his explanation and application of the *Westminster Shorter Catechism* question, 'What is effectual calling?' that Colquhoun afterwards traced his conversion.

On feeling led to devote himself to the ministry he entered Glasgow University in 1768, where he pursued his studies for ten years. The Presbytery of Glasgow licensed him to preach in 1780, and the following year he was ordained to what proved to be his only pastoral charge—the New Church in South Leith (St John's, Constitution Street). There he exercised an effective ministry until forced to give up through ill-health a year before his death in 1827.

Shortly after his conversion John Colquhoun had walked all the way from Luss to Glasgow, a distance in all of about fifty miles, to buy a copy of Thomas Boston's *Fourfold State*. This book had a moulding influence on his early Christian life. He came to esteem it next to his Bible. The influence of Boston's teaching was later to permeate his ministry and writings.

Thomas Boston's remains had been laid to rest in the beautiful churchyard of Ettrick sixteen years before Colquhoun was born, but few if any of his followers bore such marks of his influence as the minister of South Leith. Although a minister of the Established Church, Colquhoun was regarded as one of the ablest exponents of 'Marrow' theology. By an Act of Assembly on 20 May, 1720 his Church had condemned the book, *The Marrow of Modern Divinity,* because it maintained that there was a universal call and offer of the gospel to sinners. Defenders of the free offer—nicknamed 'Marrowmen' —foremost of whom were Thomas Boston and the Erskine brothers, were forced to secede from the Church in 1722. Later, however, as we find in the case of John Colquhoun, upholders of 'Marrow' teaching continued to exercise their ministry within the Establishment.

How Colquhoun reconciled his respect for an Act of the General Assembly with his uncompromising maintenance of 'Marrow' theology is illustrated in some advice he is reported to have given to the students who sought his counsel. 'Noo, ye ken', he would say to them in his colloquial tongue, 'I daurna advise ye to read the "Marrow" for the Assembly condemned it; but though they condemned the "Marrow" they didna condemn Tammes Boston's notes on the "Marrow", and that's a book that ye should read.'

It is not surprising that one of the great characteristics of Colquhoun's ministry was the emphasis on the duty and necessity of sinners complying with the offers and invitations of the gospel. At the same time he dwelt much on the danger of hypocrisy. The depth of his own spiritual experience, his discriminating views of truth, and his aptitude for religious conversation made him of great use to those in spiritual distress.

Retired and unassuming by nature, he sought no place of distinction in the Church. Indeed, it was in his mature years that he began his career as an author. He wrote seven treatises, all of which are closely related in theme and manner of presentation. The first to appear was on *Spiritual Comfort* in 1813. It was followed by *Law and Gospel* (1815), *The Covenant of Grace* (1818), *The Covenant of Works* (1822), *Saving Faith* (1824), *The Promises* (1825), and *Evangelical Repentance* (1826).

It was in his writings perhaps more than anything else that Colquhoun came nearest to Boston. They were both at their best in expounding the grand central themes of salvation, and so thoroughly had Colquhoun imbibed *The Fourfold State* that in cast of thought, mode of development, and turn of expression his own writings bear striking similarities to it. Above all, the works of both are thoroughly experimental and practical. They preached and wrote for the common people, and it was the common people of Scotland for many generations following that loved and valued their works.

The present work was originally published under the title *A View of Evangelical Repentance from the Sacred Records*, although popularly known as *Evangelical Repentance*. To avoid ambiguity the word 'Evangelical' has been dropped from the title of this reprint.

JOHN J. MURRAY
June 1965

INTRODUCTION

The Lord Jesus came not to call the righteous, but sinners to repentance. True repentance, accordingly, forms a part of the religion, not of an innocent person, but of a sinner. It is produced by the Spirit of Christ in the regeneration and sanctification of a sinner, and is absolutely essential to the character of a true Christian. As the Christian is daily sinning, he ought to be daily repenting of sin. Tertullian says, 'I was born for nothing but repentance.'

Repentance is natural, or legal, or evangelical.

Natural repentance is that natural feeling of sorrow and self-condemnation, of which a man is conscious for having done that which he sees he ought not to have done, and which arises from a discovery of the impropriety of it, or from reflecting on the disagreeable consequences of it to others, and especially to himself. This feeling of regret frequently occurs. When a man, especially a proud and vain man, is convinced of his having been guilty of some glaring instance of improper conduct, either against, or in the presence of a fellow-creature, it is sometimes very keen and painful.

Legal repentance is a feeling of regret produced in a legalist by the fear that his violations of the Divine law and especially his gross sins do expose him to eternal punishment. This regret is increased by his desire to be exempted on the ground of it from the dreadful punishment to which he knows he is condemned for them. He is extremely sorry, not that he has transgressed the law, but that the law and the justice of God are so very strict that they cannot leave him at liberty to sin with impunity. His love of sin and his hatred of holiness continue in all their vigour. And yet under the dominion of his legal temper he presumes to expect that such repentance as this will in some measure atone for all his crimes against the infinite Majesty of heaven.

Evangelical repentance is altogether different from either of these. It is a gracious principle and habit implanted in the soul by the Spirit of Christ, in the exercise of which a regenerate and believing sinner, deeply sensible of the exceeding sinfulness and just demerit of his innumerable sins is truly humbled and grieved before the Lord, on account of the sinfulness and hurtfulness of them. He feels bitter remorse, unfeigned sorrow, and deep self-abhorrence for the aggravated transgressions of his life, and the deep depravity of his nature; chiefly, because by all his innumerable provocations he has dishonoured an infinitely holy and gracious God, transgressed a law which is 'holy, and just, and good', and defiled, deformed, and even destroyed his own precious soul. This godly sorrow for sin and this holy abhorrence of it arise from a spiritual discovery of pardoning mercy with God in Christ, and from the exercise of trusting in his mercy. And these feelings and exercises are always accompanied by an unfeigned love of universal holiness, and by fixed resolutions and endeavours to turn from all iniquity to God and to walk before him in newness of life. Such, in general is the nature of that evangelical repentance, to the habit and exercise of which the Lord Jesus calls sinners who hear the gospel.

To understand spiritually and distinctly the proper place of true repentance in the covenant of grace, as well as the duty and necessity, the grace and exercise of it, is of inexpressible importance to the faith, holiness, and comfort of the Christian. It is due in a higher degree than is commonly believed, to their want of such views of it that multitudes in the visible church mistake a counterfeit for a true repentance and so flatter themselves that they are true penitents and their salvation is sure. It is because many convinced sinners have not a distinct discernment of its place in the new covenant that they apprehend that Christ will receive none but the true penitent, or that none else is warranted to trust in him for salvation. Hence, they dare not attempt coming to the gracious Redeemer till they are first satisfied that their repentance is of the *true* kind, until they can bring it as a price in their hand to procure their welcome. Instead of this, they ought without a moment's delay to come to Christ *for* true repentance. It is no less owing to their ignorance of its due place among the other blessings of salvation that many believe it to be the federal *condition* of the pardon of sin in justification, and persuade themselves that in the gospel this pardon is offered only to the penitent. And is it not because of their gross ignorance of the nature and use of true repentance that many can persuade themselves that their repentance will even atone for their crimes, that it will make satisfaction to the insulted justice of the Most High, and reinstate them in his favour? It is in a high degree owing to their ignorance of the nature and design of evangelical repentance and of its place in the new covenant that many true converts do, even for years, make their exercise of repentance a part of their warrant to renew the acting of their trust in Jesus Christ for salvation. And doubtless if others who appear to be real Christians had attained correct and distinct views of the grace, duty, and necessity of true repentance, they would not have imagined, as they seem to have done, that the exercise of it was over with their first conversion; nor would they have presumed to look back on that exercise as a ground of right to apply to themselves the unlimited offers and absolute promises of the glorious gospel.

As it is then of the utmost consequence both to sinners and to saints that they attain just and distinct views of the nature and the place of true repentance, and that they be deeply affected with the high importance and absolute necessity of it to their eternal welfare, I shall endeavour, in humble dependence on the Spirit of truth, to assist such of them as will read this treatise to attain those views. And in order the more effectually to do this, I shall consider first, the sources of true repentance; secondly, the nature and import of it; thirdly, the necessity of it; fourthly, the difference between a true and a counterfeit repentance; fifthly, the fruits or evidences of true repentance; sixthly, the priority of the acting of genuine faith to the exercise of evangelical repentance; seventhly, the priority of justification to the first exercise of true repentance; and in the last place, I shall answer some objections.

1: THE SOURCES OF TRUE REPENTANCE

In the first place, I am to consider the sources or springs of true repentance.

1. *The exercise of true or evangelical repentance flows from the work of the Holy Spirit in regeneration and sanctification.*

God has exalted Christ 'with his right hand to be a Prince and a Saviour, for to give repentance to Israel, and forgiveness of sins' (*Acts* 5:31). The Holy Spirit as the Spirit of Christ implants the principle of it in the heart at regeneration, and converts this principle into a habit in sanctification. True repentance is not the work of nature but of grace; not of a man's own spirit but of the Spirit of Christ. As it is the office of the Mediator to give repentance, so he gives it to his elect by performing these promises to them: 'I will take away the stony heart out of your flesh, and I will give you an heart of flesh' (*Ezek.* 36:36); 'I will pour upon the house of David, and upon the inhabitants of Jerusalem, the spirit of grace and of supplications; and they shall look upon me whom they have pierced, and they shall mourn for him' (*Zech.* 12:10). True repentance, which is an evangelical contrition of heart and a fixed resolution of spirit to turn from all sin to God, is wrought in the soul by the Spirit of Christ. The Spirit being given without measure to Christ, he, in the day of his power, communicates the same Spirit to his elect, who by his almighty operation breaks their hearts from and for sin, and converts them from sin to holiness. This is the primary source from which spring a true penitent's views of the malignity of sin, and his feelings of regret for it. They all result from the gracious influences of the Holy Spirit. It is his peculiar province as the Convincer of sin and misery, and the gracious Comforter to implant in the soul that holy principle, and to excite and regulate all its exercise. In producing and strengthening the habit, and in directing the exercise of this grace, the Holy Spirit commonly employs his blessed Word. he makes use of his law to break the hard heart, and of his gospel as a fire to melt it into godly sorrow for sin. 'Is not my word like as a fire? saith the Lord; and like a hammer that breaketh the rock in pieces?' (*Jer.* 23:29). Thus, the awakened sinner is on the one hand driven by the law, and on the other kindly drawn by the gospel to the exercise of sincere repentance.

2. *Meditation on or consideration of such subjects as tend by the Holy Spirit to produce and increase in the heart evangelical repentance is one of the springs of it.*

Multitudes remain impenitent for want of consideration. The Lord says, 'I hearkened and heard, but they spake not aright: no man repented him of his wickedness, saying, What have I done ?'(*Jer.* 8:6). Impenitence is in a great degree the effect of extenuating notions of the exceeding sinfulness of sin. Repentance, therefore, must spring from a deep consideration and a true sense of its infinite malignity and demerit. It flows from deep and affecting meditation on the majesty and glory, the holiness and justice, the authority and law, the threatenings and judgments of God, and on his just severity against the angels who sinned, against Adam and all his posterity, against Sodom and Gomorrah, the nations of Canaan, and the Jews, in the final destruction of their city and temple, and in the continued dispersion of their nation. These awful examples of his inexorable justice and tremendous fury show us what is his judgment of the exceeding sinfulness of sin, and of the dreadful punishment which awaits the impenitent sinner. And they are left on record that they may direct us to judge of the sin of our nature and of the transgressions of our life, as God judges. And we may be sure 'that the judgment of God is according to truth' (*Rom.* 2:2).

The exercise of true repentance flows in an eminent degree from a deep and affecting meditation on the doleful anguish and amazing death of the Lord Jesus, our adorable Surety. When we seriously consider who he was, for whom he suffered, and what he endured, we cannot but perceive God's infinite and irreconcilable abhorrence of all iniquity. Here we see that, rather than leave sin unpunished, or permit angels and men to be ignorant of his infinite detestation of that abominable thing, he would deliver up his only begotten Son, in whom his soul delighted, to the most direful anguish, agony, and death. Here we perceive that the fiery indignation of God against sin does not proceed from the smallest defect of love to sinners as his creatures, but from that infinite abhorrence of sin, which arises from a full view of its infinite malignity, and contrariety to the holiness of his nature and law. It is, then, from spiritual and heart-affecting views of the Lamb of God bearing our sins and carrying our sorrows that the exercise of evangelical repentance immediately flows. We behold in the glass of the holy and righteous law, and especially in that of the Redeemer's unparalleled sufferings, what an evil thing and bitter sin is (*Jer.* 2:19). It is not only their love of sin, but their false apprehensions of the evil and demerit of it that make sinners persist in cleaving to it. Were they to contemplate, under the enlightening influences of the Holy Spirit, the infinite malignity and desert of the sin of their nature, and of the aggravated transgressions of their life, they would flee from them with horror. Were convinced sinners but to consider seriously the heinousness of their innumerable sins, the afflictions and warnings, the counsels and reproofs, the mercies and deliverances, the light and knowledge, the obligations and vows, against which they have sinned, their eye would affect their heart, and their repentings would be kindled together (*Hos.* 11:8).

3. *The exercise of evangelical repentance, springs from a true sense of sin.*

A genuine sense of sin consists of an affecting sight, and a painful feeling, not only of the hurtfulness and danger, but also of the deformity and hatefulness of sin' (*Ezek.* 36:31). When the Holy Spirit strikes home the doctrine of the law upon the conscience, the consequence is that the sinner is instructed, and then he smites upon his thigh (*Jer.* 31:19). A true sense of sin includes an affecting sight or discernment of it by the enlightened mind. 'My sin', says the Psalmist, 'is ever before me' (*Psa.* 51:3). No sooner are the eyes of a sinner's understanding opened than he begins to see the exceeding sinfulness of sin in his heart and life. He sees his innumerable provocations, and discerns that malignity in sin which he never saw before. He sees, and is deeply affected with the sight of his great transgressions against an infinitely holy and gracious God. The holy law as a looking-glass is held before his eyes, and he therein discerns his pollution and deformity. And now that he has begun to see, he searches every corner of his heart, and every period of his life, which were before neglected as the sluggard's garden, and multitudes of secret abominations are set in the light. His mouth is stopped, and his sins at length have found him out (*Num.* 32:23). A true sense of sin also includes such a consciousness or conviction, as is a painful feeling of it. Now that the sinner is spiritually alive he has not only spiritual sight, but spiritual feeling. He begins to feel the sores of his diseased nature. The sin which sat lightly on him before becomes now a burden too heavy for him (*Psa.* 38:4). It is such a burden on his spirits, as sinks them; on his head, as it is impossible for him to discharge; and on his back, as bows it down. 'I am bowed down greatly', says the Psalmist; 'I go mourning all the day long' (*Psa.* 38:6). Accordingly, when the awakened sinner is coming to Christ, he is described as one who has a heavy burden upon him (*Matt.* 11:28). 'Take with you words, and turn to the Lord: say unto him, Take away all iniquity' [Hebrew: 'Lift off all iniquity as a burden'] (*Hos.* 14:2).

A true sense of sin is an affecting sight and feeling, especially of the exceeding sinfulness or malignity of sin. It is a sense not only of our evil doings but of the evil of our doings; not only of our sin but of the exceeding sinfulness of our sin; and not merely of things which are in themselves sinful but of the iniquity even of our holy things. The true penitent has a deep and affecting sense of the evil that cleaves even to his best performances (*Isa.* 64:6). Of all evils, he concludes that sin is the greatest, and of all sinners, he often thinks that he himself is the chief. He sees and feels that the innumerable evils which compass him about are the weightiest of burdens, the heaviest of debts, the foulest of stains, and the worst of enemies. He has a true sense of the evil of sin in reference to himself (*Rom.* 6:21), and of the evil of it with respect to God. He sees that it is the very opposite of the infinitely holy and amiable nature of God in Christ (*Hab.* 1:13). The true penitent loves God supremely, and therefore his sins are a heavy burden to him. He loathes himself because he has walked contrary to the holy Lord God, and thereby insulted, reproached, and provoked him (*Lam.* 5:16). He sees also that sin is contrary to that law of God which is holy, to that commandment which 'is holy, and just, and good (*Rom.* 7:12). Discerning the perfect equity and purity of God's law, the penitent sees the great evil of every transgression of it (*1 John* 3:4). He sees the sinfulness of sin likewise, with respect to Jesus Christ. He has an affecting discovery of it as the procuring cause of the unparalleled sufferings of his Redeemer (*Zech.* 12:10). The doleful anguish and excruciating death of the Lamb of God are comments on the evil and demerit of sin, which the penitent reads with deep attention. The dying agonies and groans of that Saviour who loved him and gave Himself for him rend his heart, and afford him the most affecting view of the evil of sin. Hence, he has such a true sense of the sinfulness of his sin, as is an abiding source of evangelical repentance.

4. *A spiritual apprehension of the pardoning mercy of God in Christ, is one of the springs of true repentance.*

Without the exercise of saving faith, or the apprehension of the mercy of God in Christ, there may be a sense of sin but not a true sense: there may be a sense of sin as hurtful to the sinner himself (*Gen.* 4:13), but not a sense of it as hateful to an holy God (*Hab.* 1:13). To apprehend the mercy of God in Christ is, to exercise the faith of his pardoning mercy. It is to rely by faith on the surety-righteousness of Jesus Christ for a right to pardon and acceptance as righteous in the sight of God, and to trust in his redeeming mercy. Accordingly the Psalmist says, 'I have trusted in thy mercy' (*Psa.* 13:5). And, again, 'I trust in the mercy of God for ever and ever' (*Psa.* 52:8). Such a knowledge of sin as is produced only by the law may result in slavish fear and worldly sorrow but it is the faith of redeeming mercy alone, as revealed and offered in the gospel, that paints iniquity in such hateful colours as to make the penitent ashamed and confounded. A deep sense of sin, indeed, may proceed from the faith of the law, but a true sense of it must arise from the faith both of the law and of the gospel. The faith of redeeming mercy is a spring of true repentance, and that by which the exercise of it is influenced and regulated. Though the graces of faith and repentance are, in respect of time, implanted together and at once; yet in order of nature, the acting of faith goes before the exercise of true repentance. The sinner then must cordially believe or trust in Christ for pardon, in order to exercise evangelical mourning for sin, and turning from it unto God. True repentance is very pleasing to God, 'but without faith it is impossible to please him (*Heb.* 11:6). To trust firmly in the Lord Jesus, both for pardon and purification, is that which, under the sanctifying influences of the Holy Spirit, will be most effectual to melt down the heart into true repentance. It is when sin is contemplated by the believer as a base and criminal outrage against the Father of mercies, and his own God and Father, that a sense of the malignity of it is deeply impressed on his heart. And it is this affecting persuasion that, by his innumerable sins, he in particular pierced the dear Redeemer; or, that the Redeemer was wounded for his transgressions, and bruised for his iniquities—it is this, I say, that melts his heart into godly sorrow and penitential mourning for his aggravated crimes (*Zech.* 12:10). It is evident then that the exercise of true repentance flows from the acting of unfeigned faith in a crucified Redeemer, and in the mercy of God through him, and that, in proportion as the acting of faith is frequent and lively, the exercise of repentance will be deep and spiritual.

These things, though they do not merit evangelical repentance, yet are the springs from which the exercise of it flows.

Is a true sense of sin one of the springs of evangelical repentance? Then it is manifest that the unconvinced sinner is not only an impenitent, but an unregenerate sinner. Reader, if ever the Holy Spirit has regenerated you, he has given you a spiritual sight and painful feeling of the sin of your nature and of the transgressions of your life. He has brought home to your conscience the precept and penalty of the Divine law as a broken covenant. The consequence has undoubtedly been that you have been truly convinced, not only of your sin, but of the malignity of your sin; not only of your evil doings, but of the evil of your doings; not merely of doings which are in themselves sinful, but

of the iniquity even of your holy things; and not only of
their desert of punishment, but of everlasting punishment.
If you never had in any degree this sense of sin, you have
never exercised true repentance. Perhaps you have been
trying to wash away your sins with the tears of a legal
repentance, but without this sense of sin you have not
exercised that repentance which is the consequence of
having washed them away in the blood of the Lamb.

Hence also it is plain that legal convictions of sin, and
legal terrors of conscience, are not true repentance. They
are sometimes introductory to the exercise of it, but they
form no part of that exercise. These are but like unripe
fruits. They must be ripened by the warm sun of Gospel-
influence, before he who has them can exercise in the
smallest degree evangelical repentance. Or rather, they
may be compared to the blossoms which appear before,
and differ in kind from the fruit. They often fall off, or go
up as dust, and no fruit of true repentance follows. The
first fruits of the second death are, alas! often mistaken
by many for the pangs of the second birth. And therefore,
if the reader has ever had them, he should examine well
whether he has experienced a deliverance out of them;
if his soul has renounced itself for justification and for
sanctification; if he has come to the Lord Jesus Christ and
him only, both for justifying righteousness, and for sanctifying grace (*Isa.* 45:24); and if his heart has been melted
and grieved for his innumerable sins, because they have
been committed against God in Christ, as a gracious God
and Father (*Jer.* 31:18). This is the harbour at which they

arrive, who come rightly out of those frightful depths. But alas! many plunge to and fro in them for a time, and land again on the same side at which they went in.

Does the exercise of evangelical repentance spring from the faith of pardoning mercy? The proper way then of dealing with the hard heart to bring it to true repentance is to press the sinner to believe in Jesus Christ for pardoning mercy and sanctifying grace. This, under the influences of the Holy Spirit, is the way to soften and melt the heart and to dispose it willingly to exercise genuine repentance. The impenitent sinner should be exhorted to imitate those fowls, which first fly up, and then dart down upon their prey; first, to soar aloft, by trusting in the redeeming mercy of God in Christ, and then, to come down in the exercise of evangelical humiliation. 'They shall look upon me whom they have pierced, and they shall mourn for him' (*Zech.* 12:10). Unbelief or distrust of pardoning mercy hardens the heart, and removes it farther and farther from God; whereas the spiritual faith of pardon touches the rebel's heart and makes it relent.

From what has been said, we may learn what a true sense of sin is. It is such a spiritual sight and feeling of sin as arises from the faith of pardoning mercy; and is such a sense of the malignity and deformity of sin as makes the penitent conclude that of all evils it is the greatest. He sees the evil of sin not only with respect to himself but with regard to God, and Christ, and the Holy Spirit. It is a distinct sense of the particular evils of the heart and life. 'Against thee, thee only have I sinned', says David, 'and done this evil in thy sight' (*Psa.* 51:4). It is a real, and not an imaginary sense of sin; and so it surpasses a merely rational conviction of sin, as far as that sense of the bitterness of gall, which is attained by tasting it, goes beyond that which is got by the bare report of it (*Jer.* 2:19). It is also an abiding, a permanent sense of iniquity. 'Mine eye', says the afflicted church, 'trickleth down, and ceaseth not, without any intermission' (*Lam.* 3:49). The removal of a plague put an end to Pharaoh's consciousness of sin, but in the true penitent the wound is deep, and so the sense is abiding. In a word, it is lively and operative. The eye of the true penitent affects his heart, and when the heart is suitably affected, it excites all the powers of the soul to action. There is a sense of sin, which discovers itself in nothing but indolent wishes, and fruitless complaints. But a true sense of it stimulates the penitent to immediate and diligent endeavours.

Hence also it is evident that it is the duty of every sinner to attain without delay a true sense of sin. For this purpose meditate frequently on such subjects as tend to beget and increase in your heart a deep sense of the odiousness and demerit of sin. Impenitence is greatly the effect of extenuating notions of the infinite malignity of transgression; whereas repentance flows from a true sense of its malignity and odiousness. Meditate also on the dreadful anguish and ignominious death of the Lamb of God, when he made Himself an offering for sin. In these you may see plainly that God's abhorrence of sin is so inexpressibly great, that he would sooner deliver up his only begotten Son, in whom his soul delighted, to the most dreadful agony and excruciating death, than leave it unpunished. To contemplate Gethsemane and Golgotha is, under the influences of the Holy Spirit, eminently conducive to evangelical repentance. Consider, too, that how light soever your crimes may sit on your spirit, they are a heavy burden to the Spirit of God. 'Behold,' says Jehovah, 'I am pressed under you, as a cart is pressed that is full of sheaves (*Amos* 2:13). The lighter that your sin lies upon your mind, the more grievous it is to the Holy Spirit of God. And if you do not sincerely repent of it, he will ease Himself of that burden, by pouring out upon you the fury of his great indignation (*Isa.* 1:24). Consider, I intreat you, that without an affecting sense of the hatefulness of sin, there is no humiliation; that without humiliation, there is no true repentance; and that without such repentance, it will be impossible for you to escape the wrath to come (*Luke* 3:13). Study then in dependence on promised grace, and that without delay, to obtain a true and a deep sense of the exceeding sinfulness of your sin.

From what has been said it is obvious that you ought also to use all the appointed means of attaining evangelical repentance. The Lord has appointed various means, and commanded you to use them. Employ them all, therefore, and instead of depending on them, or relying on your use of them, trust that the Lord Jesus will render them effectual. If you sincerely desire to repent, you will manifest your sincerity by using with diligence all appointed means. Meditate seriously then on the sin of your nature, heart, and life, and especially on the exceeding sinfulness of it. 'Remember from whence thou art fallen, and repent' (*Rev.* 2:5). Consider your ways. 'I thought on my ways', says David, 'and turned my feet unto thy testimonies' (*Psa.* 119:59). Survey minutely your inclinations and thoughts, your words and actions, even from your earliest years. Put to yourself seriously such questions as these: What have I been intending and pursuing all my days? What has been the rule of my conduct? the maxims of men, or the Word of God? the customs of the world, or the example of Christ? What has the supreme love of my heart been fixed on? Have I given to Christ, or to the world, my strongest desires and warmest attachments? Has it been my habitual intention to please God, or to please myself? Has it been his glory that I have aimed at in every pursuit, or my own gratification, wealth or honour? Is it in heaven or upon earth that I have chiefly been aiming, to lay up treasures for myself? Has God in Christ been the delightful subject of my frequent meditation and conversation? or have I regarded religious thoughts and converse as insipid and wearisome? Have I been out of my element when employed in the delightful work of prayer and praise, of reading and hearing the glorious gospel? and have I found more pleasure in licentious mirth and trifling conversation? Have I kept the Sabbath, and with holy reverence frequented the sanctuary of the Lord? or have I profaned his Sabbath, and poured contempt on his ordinances? And have I relied for all my right to eternal life on the surety-righteousness of Jesus

Christ, and trusted cordially in him for all his salvation? or have I relied for a title to life partly on my own works, and trusted in him for a part only of his salvation? Propose with impartiality these questions to yourself, and suffer conscience to return a faithful answer, in order that you may so discern your self-deformity, as to abhor yourself, and repent in dust and ashes. When you use the means, believe the promises of true repentance (*Ezek.* 36:31; *Psa.* 22:27). Upon the warrant of their being directed in offer to you, apply and trust and plead them. To believe the promises and yet not to use the means is presumption; and to use the other means and yet not to employ the principal mean of trusting Christ and the promise is self-righteousness.

When you are employing the means of evangelical repentance, be constantly on your guard against every hindrance to the exercise of it. Inconsiderateness, the not apprehending the mercy of God in Christ, slothfulness, the love and cares of the world, prejudices against the exercise of faith and the practice of holiness, and presumptuous confidence, are some of them. As these are powerful obstructions to the habit and exercise of true repentance, be always on your guard against yielding to any of them. In the faith of the promise, and with importunate supplication for the Spirit of grace, labour to mortify them.

In conclusion, it may justly be inferred from what has been advanced that it is not sound doctrine to teach that Christ will receive none but the true penitent, or that none else is warranted to come by faith to him for salvation. The regenerated sinner must first by faith embrace Christ, and apprehend the pardoning mercy of God in him before he can exercise true repentance. Accordingly, the invitations of the gospel to every sinner who hears it are these: 'Let him that is athirst, come. And whosoever will, let him take the water of life freely' (*Rev.* 22;17). 'Come ye, buy and eat; yea, come, buy wine and milk without money and without price' (*Isa.* 55:1). The evil of that doctrine is that it sets needy sinners on spinning repentance, as it were, out of their own bowels, and on bringing it with them to Christ, instead of coming to him by faith to receive it from him. It also tends to prevent convinced sinners from attempting to come to Christ, as it teaches them to keep aloof from him, till they be assured that they have true repentance to bring with them. For a sinner cannot lawfully come to the Saviour till he is sure that he has a present warrant to do so. If Jesus Christ will receive none but him who is satisfied that he has genuine repentance, then no one else is invited or commanded to believe in him; for surely, he who is invited and commanded to come to Christ will be welcome to him. Besides, if none be invited but the true penitent, then impenitent sinners are not bound to come to Christ; for none is warranted or bound to come to him, but he who is invited. And if a sinner who is not invited nor commanded does not come, he cannot be justly blamed for not coming; for where no law is, there is no transgression. The truth is that every sinner who hears the gospel is both invited and commanded to believe in the compassionate Saviour, and everyone who cordially believes in him will, in consequence, exercise evangelical repentance as a part of that salvation for which he trusts in him.

2: The Nature and Import of True Repentance

The original words in the New Testament, which, in the Authorised Version of the Bible are translated repentance, are μεταμελεια (*metameleia*) and μετανοια (*metanoia*). The former of these words signifies 'an after carefulness', or an uneasy feeling of regret and dissatisfaction for what has been done, without regard either to duration or to effects. It denotes a mere change of feeling, whether it be for the better or for the worse; such a sorrow as is not productive of a real change of conduct, and does not imply it. It does not imply a consideration either of goodness or badness, but merely of change from whatever motive or cause. It is therefore the word which is usually employed by the sacred writers to express repentance of any sort. And indeed, according to the common acceptation of the term with us, a man may as properly be said to repent of a good, as of a bad action. A covetous man will repent of the alms which a transient fit of compassion may have incited him to bestow. The original word then signifies remorse or dissatisfaction with one's self, for what one has done. On the other hand, the latter of those words signifies 'a change of mind,' of judgment, of disposition, of purpose, and of conduct. It denotes properly a change for the better; a change of mind that is not transitory, but durable, and productive of good conduct. It implies not only sorrow and remorse for what is past, but a change of disposition and of conduct for the future. When John the Baptist, our Lord, and his apostles inculcate this change of mind as a duty, or mention the necessity of it as a doctrine of Christianity, μετανοια and μετανοεω (*metanoeo*) are the terms which they invariably employ. One or other of these is the word commonly used to express the habit and exercise of that repentance which is evangelical and abiding, and not to be repented of.

The repentance then which is in the New Testament required of sinners is such an entire change of mind, or of views and sentiments respecting sin and salvation, as discovers itself by a genuine sorrow for sin, a firm resolution to hate and forsake it, and a sincere endeavour so to return to God in Christ as to walk with him in newness of life: the sincerity of which is to be evidenced by fruits meet for repentance. This, as was hinted above is true repentance. And as it is the gift of God, the purchase of Christ, and the work of the Holy Spirit, it is a saving grace. Implanted by the Spirit at regeneration, it is so inseparably connected with salvation, as to constitute an essential part of it. In the Scriptures it is called, 'repentance to salvation', and 'repentance unto life' (*Acts* 11:18); as it proceeds from, and evidences spiritual life in the soul, and as it prepares for, and issues in the perfection of life eternal; as also to distinguish it from the sorrow of the world which works death (2 *Cor.* 7:10). It is also styled, 'repentance toward God', because in the exercise of it a sinner turns from all known sin, to the love and the service of God (*Acts* 20:21).

True repentance is not a transient act, as if a sigh or a pang of sorrow for sin amounted to it. No, these may indeed be acts of true repentance, while they issue from a heart sincerely penitent: but repentance itself, instead of being a passing act, is an abiding principle, a lasting disposition of soul, a gracious principle lying deep in the heart, disposing a man at all times to mourn for and turn from sin (*Zech.* 12:10). The waters of godly sorrow for sin in the renewed heart will continue to spring up there while sin is there, though they may, through remaining hardness of heart, be much obstructed for a time. After the heart has, at the sinner's first conversion, been smitten with evangelical repentance, the wound still bleeds, and will continue more or less to bleed until the band of glory be put about it in the holy place on high. If, therefore, a man regards repentance only as the first stage in the way to heaven, and instead of renewing daily his exercise of it, satisfies himself with concluding that he has passed the first stage, the truth of his repentance is very questionable. The man who does not see his need of exercising repentance daily may have a counterfeit, but cannot have a true repentance. He may have a superficial sorrow for his sins, and even such remorse gnawing his conscience as may be the first moving of the worm that shall never die, as that of Judas was, and yet be a total stranger to that evangelical repentance, which is both a saving grace and an abiding principle.

In the heart of the true penitent, a wonderful and permanent change has been graciously effected. He is irresistibly constrained to abandon his former views of sin, of salvation from sin, and of the pleasantness and beauty of holiness, and to embrace sentiments altogether opposite. Such a change is produced in his inclinations and affections that he no longer takes pleasure in unrighteousness, but delights in the law of God and in obedience to it after the inward man. And the more pleasure he takes in holiness, the more deep, and even delicious will his sorrow for sin be, and the more vigorous will his endeavours be to turn from all sin to God. And yet, so far is he from meriting any blessing from God by his exercise of true repentance, that he is laid under fresh obligations to him for having granted to him the inestimable blessing of repentance unto life. The more of it he receives from God, the more he is bound to honour him by a lively and a frequent exercise of it.

Having thus glanced at the formal nature of evangelical repentance, I now proceed to consider, what the exercise of it includes.

In the first place, It imports deep humiliation of soul before the Lord.

It is by the high way of pride that sinners depart from God; and it is by the low way of humiliation that they return to him. The grace of Christ brings elect sinners down from their high conceit of themselves and lays them low at the footstool of a gracious God. It makes them humble themselves under the mighty hand of God that he may exalt them in due time (*1 Pet.* 5:6). As it was with Benhadad's servants (*1 Kings* 20:31-32), so it is with true penitents. By faith, they understand that the King of Israel is a merciful King; by repentance, they put sackcloth on their loins, and ropes on their heads, and in that humble posture, they come to him. Evangelical humiliation is the immediate consequence of a true sense of sin, and of a spiritual apprehension of pardoning mercy. It consists in lowliness, or self-abasement of mind before God, and esteeming others better than ourselves; in having low thoughts of ourselves, and a deep sense of our extreme meanness, hatefulness, weakness, and unworthiness in the sight of God. It is the sense that a true Christian has of his own despicableness, odiousness on account of sin, and utter inability for the least good thought, word, or work, and that with a suitable frame of heart.

In true humiliation the believing sinner sees the hatefulness of his iniquity, and the inexpressible odiousness of his heart and life because of sin; and he has an answerable frame of spirit, a disposition to abhor and abase himself as a sinner, to exalt Christ alone, and voluntarily to deny and renounce himself. The hypocritical or legal penitent is lifted up with an high opinion of his humiliation, and is ostentatious of it; whereas the true penitent is deeply humbled for the pride of his heart. He accounts himself one of the least of saints, and is disposed to think others better than himself (*Phil.* 2:3). He sees that his humiliation is very small in comparison of what it ought to be, and that his pride is very great and exceeding sinful. He is a thousand times more quick-sighted in discerning his pride and self-righteous temper than his humility. On the contrary, the hypocrite is blind to nothing so much as to his pride, and quick-sighted to nothing so much as to his show of humility. Evangelical humiliation then is a principal part of the exercise of true repentance. The sincere penitent so discerns and feels the plague of his own heart as to think less favourably of himself than he can do of others, or they of him.

Secondly, The exercise of true repentance includes godly sorrow for sin.

The remorse of the evangelical penitent is a sorrowful remorse, a deep contrition of heart, not so much for the punishment to which he has exposed himself, as for the indignity he has done to a holy, a gracious, and a merciful God, The apostle Paul styles it, 'Sorrow according to God,' or 'godly sorrow' (2 *Cor.* 7:10), not only to distinguish it from the sorrow of the world which works death, but to show that it is grief for sin because it is sin; because it is an infinite offence given, and an infinite dishonour done, to a holy, a good, and a gracious God, a transgressing of his holy and righteous law, a defacing of his moral image, a piercing of his dear Son, and a grieving of his Holy Spirit. Trusting that the spotless Lamb of God was pierced for his iniquities, the true penitent mourns, not so much for himself as for him (*Zech.* 12:10). And so real, so deep is his penitential sorrow that though there were no conscience to accuse, no judge to condemn, no devil to affright, no hell to torment, yet he would mourn and be in bitterness for having offended that God who has loved him, pierced that Saviour who died for him, and grieved that Spirit who sanctifies and comforts him. 'Against thee, thee only have I sinned', says the Psalmist, 'and done this evil in thy sight' (*Psa.* 51:4). His penitential sorrow springs, not only from a true sense of the infinite hatefulness of his innumerable sins, but also from the faith of redeeming mercy, and from his love of God and of his holy law.

His godly sorrow springs likewise from his views of the infinite majesty, excellence, holiness, and amiableness of that transcendently glorious God whom he has insulted; of the injustice and base ingratitude of which he has been guilty; and of the infinite obligations to obedience which he has violated. Now that his views of sin are changed, he feels deep regret, bitter remorse, and intense sorrow for what he has done against his gracious God and Father. His iniquities appear to his mind inexpressibly odious, and they become a heavy burden, too heavy for him. He mourns bitterly for them, and still mourns that he cannot mourn more. His heart is broken, and as it were melted when he considers the odiousness and the multitude of his crimes against that gracious God, who all the time was full of infinite love to him. He grieved the Holy Spirit by committing sin, and he himself is now grieved in repenting of it. The adamantine heart is dissolved into tears of godly sorrow; the rock is struck by the rod of evangelical truth, and the waters gush out. This is that rending of the heart, which the Lord requires (*Joel* 2:12-13).

The sorrow of evangelical repentance is inward and real sorrow. It is not a bowing down of the head as a bulrush (*Isa.* 58:5), nor a disfigured countenance. It rises from inward principles of faith and love; and so it makes the man mourn in secret before the Lord. It is deep sorrow, sorrow which descends deeply into the heart. To dig deep was the security of the house that was founded upon a rock (*Luke* 6:48). Penitential sorrow is a pricking or piercing of the heart as with spears and swords, or a compunction of heart (*Acts* 2:37). But is godly sorrow deeper in the heart than the deepest grief on any worldly account? If we calculate merely by feeling, or by the moving of the affections, it is plain that it does not always appear deeper than other sorrows. But if we compute by the fixed disposition of the heart, it is evident that it is deeper than them all, and exceeds the greatest of them. Persons are usually moved more sensibly by a less degree of sorrow than by a greater. The greatest grief is often above tears.

Penitential sorrow settles more deeply, and continues more firm than any other grief.

It is also a lively sorrow, a grief that quickens the soul. The sorrow of the world works death; it indisposes a man for activity in duty. But godly sorrow, quickens a man to the spiritual performance of duty (2 *Cor.* 7:11). The former arises from slavish dread, which chills and stiffens the soul, and so renders it unfit for action, the latter from faith and love, which warm the heart, and dispose it to be ardent and active (*Luke* 7:47).

It is a universal sorrow. The evangelical penitent is grieved in heart not only for his own iniquities but for those of others (*Psa.* 119:136). He never mourns sincerely for any one sin who does not mourn for all; and he never grieves aright for the iniquities of his life who does not bewail bitterly the sin of his nature.

It is moreover an operative sorrow. It 'worketh repentance to salvation, not to be repented of' (2 *Cor.* 7:10). Godly sorrow and turning to God are inseparable. Evangelical sorrow in the heart is a spring which, as it runs, works out the love, power, and practice of sin. In a word, it is sorrow which continues in the heart as long as sin remains in it. The grief of the legal penitent is like a summer flood, which is soon over, but the sorrow of the evangelical penitent is like a living spring, which, in a greater or lesser measure, always sends forth water.

In the third place, Another ingredient in the exercise of true repentance is hatred of all sin, accompanied by self-loathing.

True hatred of sin, under the sanctifying influences of the Holy Spirit, flows from faith working by love to God; and it is a holy abhorrence of every sin as infinitely hateful to him. This hatred is universal against all sin, whether it be known or unknown. 'I hate,' says the Psalmist, 'every false way' (*Psa.* 119:104). It is irreconcilable to any known sin. 'I hate the work of them that turn aside', says the Psalmist again, 'it shall not cleave to me' (*Psa.* 101:2). It is constant without intermission. It is a hearty detestation, an utter abhorrence of all sin as sin, and of every appearance of sin; an utter abhorrence of it as peculiarly odious, as inexpressibly abominable; a detestation of it in its nature as the greatest of all evils, the worst of all enemies, as the most inveterate enemy, not only of the precious soul, but of that God whose nature is infinitely lovely and loving. The more the true penitent is enabled to trust that Jesus was wounded for his transgressions and was bruised for his iniquities, the more he abhors them. In the sufferings and death of the Lamb of God, he sees what infinite wrath, what tremendous punishment he as a sinner deserves. And when he cordially trusts that the Lord Jesus so loved him, as willingly to endure all that punishment for him, his iniquities appear inexpressibly hateful in his view, and he longs to be able to hate them with perfect hatred. He abhors sin as the worst of all evils, worse even than the evil of suffering: and were he left to his choice, without fear of ever being called to account, he would not choose sin; for he abhors it, because of its contrariety to the holy nature and law of God.

True hatred of sin is accompanied by self-loathing. 'Then shall ye remember your own evil ways, and your doings that were not good, and shall loathe yourselves in your own sight for your iniquities, and for your abominations' (*Ezek.* 36:31). The true penitent loathes, not only the sin which dwells in him, and the innumerable transgressions which have been committed by him, but he loathes himself as a sinner. Seeing in the glass of the loving-kindness, sparing mercy, and holy law of God, and of the agony and anguish of his Redeemer, the unutterable deformity, odiousness and demerit of his sins, he abhors himself for his iniquities and abominations. 'Wherefore I abhor myself', says Job, 'and repent in dust and ashes' (*Job* 42:6). He does not indeed loathe himself as a creature, but he loathes himself as a sinner. He looks on himself as a most deformed, a most polluted object. He now rejects with holy indignation all the vain excuses for sin which he used formerly to make, and with which he satisfied his conscience. He accuses, judges, and condemns himself. He is accordingly represented as smiting on his breast (*Luke* 18:13); thereby declaring that he considers his depraved heart within to be the source of all his other abominations, and that he justly deserves to be struck at the heart and to die for his innumerable and aggravated crimes. He sees now that his heart and his life are a most loathsome spectacle; all as an unclean thing, and that all his righteousnesses are as filthy rags. He loathes himself, therefore, and renounces all confidence in himself.

Fourthly, The exercise of true repentance includes shame and confusion of face before the Lord.

The remembrance of his innumerable, and heinous provocations fills the true penitent with holy shame and blushing before God. 'O my God', says Ezra, 'I am ashamed and blush to lift up my face to thee, my God; for our iniquities are increased over our head, and our trespass is grown up unto the heavens' (*Ezra* 9:6). Shame was never felt in the world till our first parents had lost their reputation by sinning against God. It is in consequence of a true sense of sin, and of a fiducial apprehension of pardoning mercy that the true penitent is filled with shame before a holy and gracious God, for the deep depravity of his nature and the aggravated transgressions of his life.

Spiritual nakedness also occasions shame. Accordingly Adam, after he had sinned, said to the Lord, 'I heard thy voice in the garden; and I was afraid, because I was naked, and I hid myself' (*Gen.* 3:10). Sin has taken away the comeliness of human nature. It has stripped the sinner of his beautiful garments, so that the shame of his nakedness appears. The believing sinner sees that, and has this great promise fulfilled to him: 'That thou mayest remember, and be confounded, and never open thy mouth any more because of thy shame, when I am pacified toward thee for all that thou hast done, saith the Lord God' (*Ezek.* 16:63). Reproach causes shame. 'Sin is a reproach to any people' (*Prov.* 14:34). That knowledge of sin which is by the law may produce worldly sorrow, but it is the province of the gospel only to paint sin in such colours as to make the true penitent ashamed, yea, even confounded because he bears the reproach of his youth (*Jer.* 31:19). A true sense especially of base ingratitude, when it is accompanied by the faith of redeeming mercy fills him with shame: 'We lie down in our shame, and our confusion covereth us; for we have sinned against the Lord our God' (*Jer.* 3:25). The disappointment also of his former hopes from sin fills the penitent with holy shame. During his unregenerate state he expected satisfaction and happiness in a course of disobedience, but now that his views of sin are changed, he sees that he was all the time procuring for himself nothing but present misery and endless destruction. His reflection upon this often fills him with shame. Accordingly, the apostle Paul puts this question: 'What fruit had ye then in those things whereof ye are now ashamed? for the end of those things is death' (*Rom.* 6:21). A spiritual discovery also of the pollution of his sin fills the penitent with shame. Sin defiles as well as deforms the soul in the sight of God. The true penitent sees this and is ashamed. 'We are all as an unclean thing', says the church, 'and all our righteousnesses are as filthy rags (*Isa.* 64:60). And Daniel explains, 'O Lord, righteousness belongeth unto thee, but unto us, confusion of faces, as at this day' (*Dan.* 9:7).

In the fifth place, *The exercise of true repentance implies ingenuous and unreserved confession of sin to the glory of that God who has been dishonoured by it.*

Thus Joshua exhorted Achan, 'My son, give glory to the Lord God of Israel, and make confession unto him' (*Josh.* 7:19). This is the way in which the true penitent vents his godly sorrow, self-loathing, and shame. 'I acknowledged my sin unto thee', says the Psalmist, 'and mine iniquity have I not hid: I said, I will confess my transgressions unto the Lord; and thou forgavest the iniquity of my sin' (*Psa.* 32:5). If the sin has been committed in secret, confession to God in secret will suffice. If it has been a private offence, given not only to God but to a fellow-creature, the confession is to be made not merely to God, but to that fellow-creature in private (*James* 5:16). If it has been a public offence, the confession should be public likewise (*1 Tim.* 5:20). Accordingly, David published his confession to the church (*Psa.* 51), and so did Paul (*1 Tim.* 1:13). As the secret confession is to be made to God only, so the private and public confessions, are to be made to him chiefly. Ingenuous confession of sin is so necessary in the exercise of true repentance that in Scripture it is put for the whole of repentance. Thus saith the Lord, 'I will go and return to my place, till they acknowledge their offence' (*Hos.* 5:15).

The true penitent by his unreserved confession of his crimes accuses himself. With sorrow and shame he confesses to the honour of his God and Father, that times without number he has transgressed his holy and righteous law. 'I acknowledge my transgressions', says David, 'and my sin is ever before me' (*Psa.* 51:3). He also condemns himself. When he looks into the holy law and considers the infinite malignity and demerit of his innumerable crimes, he reads his doom and passes sentence on himself. 'Father', said the returning prodigal, 'I have sinned against heaven and before thee, and am no more worthy to be called thy son' (*Luke* 15:18-19). He sees and confesses that he deserves for his great and aggravated provocations to sink throughout eternity under the overwhelming wrath of almighty God. And he says with the afflicted church, 'It is of the Lord's mercies that I am not consumed' (*Lam.* 3:22). He sees that it would have been just with God to have punished him, considered as in himself, with everlasting destruction. Instead of covering his transgression as Adam, the true penitent knows not where to find expressions strong enough to set forth the extreme malignity of the very least of his crimes. He lays his hand upon his mouth, and his mouth in the dust, as being unable to declare either the multitude of his iniquities or the greatness of their aggravations. His confession, accordingly, is free, sincere, particular, and habitual.

Lastly, The exercise of evangelical repentance, includes the sinner's turning from all sin to God in Christ.

This is the formal nature of true repentance, or that which completes it. It is under this notion of it that evangelical repentance is, in the Old Testament, often styled 'returning' or 'conversion'. In the exercise of this repentance the convinced sinner returns and comes to himself (*Luke* 15:17); and then he turns from all sin to God. Whenever he comes to himself, he will come to Christ by faith, and to God in him by repentance.

1. True penitents turn from all sin. 'Repent, and turn from your idols, and turn away your faces from all your abominations' (*Ezek.* 14:6). To continue in the practice of sin is inconsistent with the exercise of true repentance.

Sincere penitents cease from sin. Though sin remains in them, yet it does not reign as formerly. Though they cannot shake themselves loose of the remains of sin, yet they turn from it, both in their heart and in their life.

They turn from all sin in heart and affection. Although iniquity still cleaves to them, yet they no longer cleave to it as formerly, but detest and loathe it (*Rom.* 7:24). Sin still hangs on them, but it is only as chains on the captive, which are his grievous burden; or, as the grave-clothes on Lazarus, when he was raised from the dead, which he was trying to shake off. Their esteem and love of sin are changed into hatred of it. 'I hate vain thoughts', says the Psalmist (*Psa.* 119:113). And again, 'I hate every false way' (*Psa.* 119:104). In the exercise of true repentance their hearts are turned against all iniquity, and they abhor it as the worst of evils, worse than even the most exquisite suffering. Instead of taking pleasure in sin as formerly, they now loathe it. Hence the exercise of such repentance is styled, a casting away of all their transgressions (*Ezek.* 18:31); as one would cast away some very loathsome thing, which he cannot endure to be near him. 'Thou shalt cast them away as a menstruous cloth; thou shalt say unto it, Get thee hence' (*Isa.* 30:22). In a word, their cleaving to sin is turned into an ardent and increasing desire to be free from it. Though formerly sin was dear to them as the apple of the eye; yet now that their heart is rent from it, as well as for it, they long vehemently to be delivered from it. Thus they turn from the love of all sin in their heart.

True penitents turn also from all sin in their life, or external conduct. They study to have clean hands as well as a pure heart. In the exercise of repentance they refuse compliance with the corrupt desires of the flesh and of the mind; and so, they through the Spirit mortify the members and deeds of the body of sin (*Rom.* 8:13). They turn from gross sins, or outward abominations. They may indeed be left on some occasion to fall into a gross sin, as David and Peter were, but they are not suffered, as the impenitent are, to lie in it. They are raised again by repentance. 'A just man falleth seven times, and riseth up again' (*Prov.* 24:16). They watch habitually against all temptations to sin (*Psa.* 18:23), and all occasions of it (*Prov.* 4:14-15); and in proportion to the degree of their sanctification, they abstain even from all appearance of evil. They not only turn from the practice of open and gross sin, but they strive daily against the sins of common infirmity. They exercise themselves, 'to have always a conscience void of offence toward God, and toward men' (*Acts* 24:16). Their conscience is tender with respect to secret as well as to open sins; and therefore they are as deeply concerned to resist motions of sin, and temptations to it in secret before the Lord, as to strive against sinful words and actions openly before the world. And when through infirmity any of them is overtaken in a fault, he, under the sanctifying influences of the Holy Spirit, renews his exercise of faith and repentance, and so he is always departing from iniquity. True penitents will always be repenting as long as sin remains in them and prevails against them.

They who consider turning from sin as the work only of a few days or weeks at a man's first conversion are not true penitents. As evangelical repentance is included in sanctification, and as turning from sin both in heart and life is the same as dying to sin, the evangelical penitent is, in principle and practice, constantly turning from sin.

2. True penitents turn from all sin to God in Christ. They departed from God by sin: they return to him by repentance. 'Come, and let us return unto the Lord' (*Hos.* 6:1). This is the term to which sinners turn in evangelical repentance. Many who profess repentance turn from one sin to another and never to God: 'They return, but not to the most High (*Hos.* 7:16). But when the Holy Spirit enables sinners to trust in Christ for that salvation of which pardon of sin and repentance are essential parts, he thereby turns them from all sin to God; and when they are thus turned, they turn to him. 'Turn thou me, and I shall be turned . . . Surely after that I was turned, I repented' (*Jer.* 31:18-19). By faith sinners return to God as their God and portion, and through Christ take up their everlasting rest in him as the strength of their heart, and their portion for ever. But by repentance they return to the love of him as their Lord or Master, and to their duty to him as such.

In the exercise of evangelical repentance they turn to the love of God as their Lord and Master. 'O Lord our God, other lords besides thee have had dominion over us; but by thee only will we make mention of thy name' (*Isa.* 26:13). They account him infinitely worthy to be obeyed, and served, and pleased in all things. They see the transcendent glory, and amiableness of God in Christ, and therefore they count him infinitely worthy of all the love of their hearts, and of all the worship and obedience of their lives (*James* 2:7). They testify their supreme love of him by a deliberate and cordial choice of him as their only Lord. 'Then shall she say, I will go and return to my first husband; for then was it better with me than now' (*Hos.* 2:7). They discern the excellence and amiableness, not only of the Lord God Himself, but also of his laws and ordinances, his image and service; and, therefore, they firmly resolve to cleave to him and serve him. They also testify their love of him, by regarding his service as the greatest freedom, the highest honour, and the truest happiness. When the prodigal came to himself, he said, 'How many hired servants of my father's, have bread enough and to spare' (*Luke* 18:17). To the same purpose the Psalmist says, 'Blessed are they that dwell in thy house: they will be still praising thee' (*Psa.* 84:4). All true penitents consider the service of sin as the greatest bondage, the deepest misery, but the service of God in Christ as the truest freedom, the sweetest happiness. Their minds have been enlightened to see the deformity of sin and the beauty of holiness, and therefore their hearts abhor the one, and delight in practising the other.

True penitents turn also to their duty to God as their Lord and Master. When Saul of Tarsus became a penitent, he said, 'Lord what wilt thou have me to do?' (*Acts* 9:6). All who return to God come home as servants to do his work. All who become his friends do whatsoever he commands them (*John* 15:14). They 'delight in the law of God after the inward man', and have respect to all his commandments. As it is with their whole heart that they return to the love and practice of their duty, so they have a full and fixed purpose of heart in dependence on the grace of Christ, to yield new obedience to God. 'O Lord, I have said that I would keep thy words.' 'I have inclined my heart to perform thy statutes alway, even unto the end' (*Psa.* 119:57, 112). They return to their duty, with a full purpose to enter upon and keep the way of duty; to pursue and practise holiness in all manner of conversation. This full purpose is a sincere resolution to return to the practice of every known duty. True penitents study to know what is duty in every situation, and when it is known, to perform it. They endeavour to serve the Lord cheerfully and diligently in heart and in life.

It is also a purpose to return to spirituality in every duty. 'We are the circumcision', says the apostle, 'which worship God in the spirit' (*Phil* 3:3). Sincere penitents resolve through grace to have their hearts as well as their hands engaged in their duties; to perform them from union with Christ, faith, and love as the principles; from the grace of God and the love of Christ as the motives; in the strength of the grace of Christ, and with the whole heart as the manner; and to the glory of God in Christ as the ultimate end of them. This resolution is usually called a full purpose because it is a resolution which is put in execution without delay. 'I made haste', says the Psalmist, 'and delayed not, to keep thy commandments' (*Psa.* 119:60). It is so called also because a sincere endeavour after new obedience is inseparably connected with it. Although true penitents are sensible that they cannot in their own strength perform new obedience, yet they habitually aim at it, and even at perfection in it (*Phil.* 3:14). The obedience which they purpose and endeavour to yield is styled new obedience because the principles, the motives, the rule, the manner, and the end of it are all new.

The true penitent's turning from all sin to God is voluntary. Some turn from their sins sore against their will. They part from their darling sins with great reluctance, as the covetous man from his possessions at death, when he is forced to let them go. The true penitent, on the contrary, turns from all iniquity with willingness, or by choice. In the same manner does he turn to God. He voluntarily and heartily yields himself to him, to serve him. 'Thy people shall be willing in the day of thy power' (*Psa.* 110:3). His turning from all sin is also sincere. He turns from iniquity, not so much because it is hurtful, but because it is hateful to him. He departs from it because it offends an infinitely holy and gracious God, dishonours his dear Son, grieves his Holy Spirit, violates his law, and defaces his image. His return to God in Christ is sincere. He turns to him, not feignedly but with his whole heart (*Jer.* 3:10). Hypocrites have a divided heart, one part for God and another for sin. But 'No man can serve two masters.' Moreover, he turns speedily from sin to God. As long as a man delays to turn from all sin his repentance is feigned. A true penitent will no more delay, than a man would to snatch a burning coal from his bosom. He will not delay a moment. He will make no truce with sin. He knows that if he delay a single moment longer it may prove fatal to him. He therefore imitates the Psalmist, who says, 'I made haste, and delayed not, to keep thy commandments' (*Psa.* 119:60).

His turning from sin is also universal. Whoever turns sincerely from any sin turns from all sin. Accordingly, Jehovah gave this command to the house of Israel: 'Cast away from you all your transgressions' (*Ezek.* 18:31). One sin retained would render all his exercise of repentance vain; just as Abimelech, the son of Jerubbaal's concubine, was the death of all his seventy sons by his wives, except one (*Judg.* 8:29-9:5). The true penitent, therefore, abstains from all appearance of evil, and carefully avoids every avenue of temptation. Every sin as such is the object of his deep abhorrence. And if any iniquity has prevailed against him more than another, if any sin has easily beset him, this he resolutely and cheerfully foregoes, and with unreluctant mind abandons. He so abandons every known sin as to return to the love, and to the spiritual performance of every known duty. He not only yields new obedience, but attempts the performance of it in all its parts.

So much for the nature and import of true repentance.

From what has been said it may justly be inferred that

there is no exercise of true repentance without a heart broken from and for sin. Sinners either must be broken-hearted for their sins, and be mourners in Zion, or God will break them with the rod of his fiercest indignation. They either must be of a contrite, that is, of a bruised or crushed spirit for the unnumbered sins of their heart and life, or God will crush them under the overwhelming weight of his unsupportable wrath. They will either mourn and be in bitterness for their great transgressions, in time, or they shall weep and wail under the punishment of them, through eternity. Alas! there are multitudes of sinners at this day who are stout-hearted, who boldly out face reproofs, both from the Word of God and their consciences, with hearts that neither break nor bow. O that such would seriously reflect that a day shall come in which God will make the stoutest heart to tremble, and the hardest heart to fly as in a thousand pieces! 'Thou shalt break them with a rod of iron,' says the Psalmist: 'Thou shalt dash them in pieces like a potter's vessel' (*Psa.* 2:9). 'Who knoweth the power of thine anger?' (*Psa.* 90:11). Some secure sinner will say, 'I daily repent of my sins.' Well would it be with you if you did so indeed. But no one is so ready to pretend that he has true repentance as he who is yet an utter stranger to it. If some regret for your sins and a transient wish for mercy were true repentance, it were easy work. But it is far, very far from being so. You cannot repent evangelically or acceptably without a new heart, a broken and contrite spirit, a heart broken from and for all your iniquity. Neither can you do so without cordial trust in the pardoning mercy of God in Christ. Be exhorted, O impenitent sinner, to exercise that godly sorrow for sin which is a fruit of saving faith, and which worketh repentance to salvation. Be no longer a stranger to the exercise of evangelical mourning for the innumerable evils of your heart and life. 'Blessed are they that mourn, for they shall be comforted' (*Matt.* 5:4).

It is also evident from what has been stated that sin will be followed by shame, either in this world or in that which is to come. If a sinner live and die without true repentance, his shame in the eternal world is certain. He shall be covered with shame before all the armies of heaven and all the generations of the children of Adam at the last day, and with the most overwhelming shame in the place of torment for ever and ever. 'Many of them that sleep in the dust of the earth, shall awake . . . some to shame and everlasting contempt' (*Dan.* 12:2). And if the sinner is enabled, before it is too late, to exercise repentance unto life, he will be covered with holy shame and blushing before the Lord. He will glorify God by taking shame to himself for the loathsome deformity and pollution of his unholy nature and life. If by the eye of faith he discerns that mercies and forgivenesses belong to the Lord, he will surely confess that to himself belongs confusion of face. If he is enabled to trust cordially that the Lord is pacified toward him for all that he has done, he will remember and be confounded and never open his mouth any more, because of his shame (*Ezek.* 16:63). He will in secret before God be ashamed even of that which no fellow-creature could ever witness. He will be as much ashamed of secret, as of open abominations.

We may hence infer also that shamelessness in sinning is a sure mark of impenitence; and is therefore a forerunner of everlasting shame (*Jer.* 16:15; *Phil.* 3:19). Impudence in committing sin reveals a hard and impenitent heart, and a seared conscience. Ah! what well-grounded hope of heavenly glory can that man have who glories in his shame, and who, instead of being ashamed of having sinned, would be ashamed of appearing penitent?

Sin must surely be a very loathsome object in the eyes of the true penitent, since the sight of it makes him loathe himself. No man truly abhors his sins but he who loathes and abhors himself as a sinner. An impenitent sinner usually loves that in himself which he appears to loathe in others, but the true penitent loathes sin in himself even more than he does in others. And when he loathes himself in his own sight for having sinned against an infinitely holy and gracious God, it is at once a part and an evidence of his being a true penitent; an argument that his love of sin is turned into hatred of it. If a person, then, wishes to attain true self-loathing, let him in the faith of illuminating and renewing influences, look narrowly into himself. Let him closely and frequently inspect the inexpressible malignity and deformity of the sin that dwells in him and of the innumerable abominations that are committed by him. Many a poor sinner is pining away in his iniquity and in all the loathsomeness of inbred corruption, threatening his eternal perdition, whilst in the mean time he is fond of his condition and is dreaming of happiness. But, if sovereign mercy prevent it not, dreadful shall be his surprise when he awakes in the place of torment. O let no sinner remain a stranger to the exceeding sinfulness of his heart and life! Let everyone consider seriously and frequently the infinite odiousness and demerit of his transgressions and his extreme need of union and communion with the Lord Jesus Christ.

Does evangelical repentance include confession of sin? Let the reader, then, study to be sincere, free, full, and particular in confessing his iniquities to the Lord. Your debt by nature and practice to the law and the justice of God is boundless. You can accumulate, but you cannot pay the immense sum. You are utterly insolvent. If you be not found in Christ as Jehovah our Righteousness, you owe to the holy law as a covenant of works a debt of perfect obedience for life, and of infinite satisfaction for sin. Confess then the infinite sum. Confess it to the Lord in order to prevent a legal pursuit, and to be capable of praying consistently for a remission of it, which otherwise you cannot be. O if you had a spiritual sense of your aggravated sins and godly sorrow for them, these like an overflowing torrent would bear down before them all those things which now indispose you for a free and particular confession of them.

Is evangelical repentance a turning from all sin to God in Christ? Let the reader then examine himself, whether he has, in heart and affection, turned from all iniquity. Is your esteem of all sin turned into contempt and dislike of it? Is your love of every sin turned into abhorrence of it, and into self-loathing because of it? Is your cleaving to any darling, any predominant lust, changed into a longing to be perfectly and eternally freed from it? Have you turned from all known sin in your external conduct? Have you forsaken all gross pollutions? Are you habitually on your guard against all sins even of common infirmity, abstaining from all appearances of evil? Do you labour, in dependence on promised grace, to resist the motions of sin in your heart, and to refuse compliance with them in your life? Is your turning from all sin, voluntary and sincere? Have you returned to God in Christ? Instead of turning from one sin to another, have you returned from all iniquity to the Lord? Do you esteem him worthy to be obeyed, served, and pleased in all things? Do you choose him as your only Lord, and regard his service as your greatest happiness, your highest honour? Have you with your heart returned to your duty to him? Is your heart reconciled to the whole law of God, the whole yoke of Christ? Have you in your heart a deliberate and full purpose of new obedience? Have you returned to the cheerful practice of every known duty, and to spirituality in all? Have you returned to the performance of every duty, voluntarily, sincerely, and without delay? Is it in the faith of pardoning mercy and of sanctifying grace that you endeavour to perform all your duties? If you have been enabled in any measure to do so, you may be satisfied that you are a true penitent. And though your consciousness of being such is no part of your warrant for renewing your actings of faith in the Lord Jesus, yet it will be an encouragement to you to renew them upon the warrant afforded you in the glorious gospel. But if you are still not satisfied that you are a true penitent, come as a sinner to him who is exalted to give repentance, and trust in him for that evangelical repentance which is a substantial part of spiritual life, of that life which is founded on justification, carried on by sanctification, and completed in glorification.

Is repentance a turning of the heart from all sin? It plainly follows that turning from sin outwardly, while the heart still cleaves to it, is far from being true repentance. It is easy indeed to reform outwardly, but the great business consists in getting the heart, by justifying and regenerating grace, broken from and for all manner of sin. If you would be satisfied, that your repentance is not counterfeit but true, you must examine the motives which excite you to turn from iniquity. For the low and legal motives which rise no higher than yourself, your own safety and welfare, will never evidence you to be a true penitent.

Many, alas! cease from certain acts of sin merely because sin ceases from them. They have not left sin, but some particular sin has quit them. Many an old sinner thinks himself a true penitent because he is not disposed as formerly to wallow in the mire of youthful lusts. Some forsake certain sins, but not from the evangelical principles of saving faith in the great Redeemer, union with him, love to him, and hatred of all sin as sin. They do not love supremely the holy nature of God in Christ, and therefore they do not hate the nature of sin. But they can never begin to exercise evangelical repentance till they hate the very nature of all iniquity, and begin to turn from it with holy abhorrence because it is hateful not only to God but to themselves. Every sin is, in its very nature, most detestable to the true penitent.

It follows also that merely negative reformation is not true repentance. A man must not only turn from all sin, but turn to God. The evangelical penitent not only ceases to do evil but learns to do well (*Isa.* 1:16-17). He not only abhors that which is evil but cleaves to that which is good (*Rom.* 12:9). He not only mortifies his corrupt inclinations and affections, but he possesses and exercises the contrary graces. Many reform externally from the evils of their past life, but they do not go forward to the ways of faith and holiness. Like the proud Pharisee, who went up to the temple to pray, they satisfy themselves with being not unjust, not extortioners, not adulterers. But they do not consider that no sooner is the house from which the unclean spirit is gone out, empty, than he returns with seven other spirits more wicked than himself, and they enter in and dwell there; and so the last state of that man is worse than the first (*Matt.* 12:44-45). In evangelical repentance, the regenerate and believing sinner returns from the love and practice of sin to the love and enjoyment of God, and to that new obedience to him which flows from faith and love. Turning to God in Christ is the essence of evangelical repentance.

In conclusion, the exercise of repentance must be the

work of our whole lives, for so our turning from sin and returning to God will be, if we are true penitents. While the sincere penitent is fleeing from sin, it follows him. It often overtakes him, and therefore he must renew his flight often. New provocations require a renewed exercise of repentance; nay, old sins are not to be forgotten. 'Remember', said Moses to Israel, 'and forget not, how thou provokedst the Lord thy God to wrath in the wilderness' (*Deut.* 9:7). And the Psalmist prayed thus: 'Remember not the sins of my youth, nor my transgressions' (*Psa.* 25:7). The whole life of the true penitent is a continual warfare. During this warfare he must fight many battles. Sometimes he gains the victory and sometimes he loses. If he loses he must renew the fight: if he gains, he must pursue the victory and prepare for a new encounter. But he should always be of good courage and maintain his conflicts resolutely, for though he may lose a particular battle, yet he shall be more than a conqueror at last (*Rom.* 8:37).

3: THE NECESSITY OF TRUE REPENTANCE

By the necessity of repentance is meant the need that a sinner has of it, as that which is indispensably requisite for him. A sinner must either repent or perish. He acts most unjustly, as well as unreasonably, if he continue impenitent. Besides, he is under infinite obligations to repent. Now true repentance is necessary, or indispensably requisite, chiefly on the following accounts:

1. *It is necessary because the Lord in his holy law has peremptorily required it.*

It is one of the duties required in the first commandment of the moral law.[1] It is more expressly commanded, both in the Old Testament and in the New. 'Thus saith the Lord GOD, Repent and turn yourselves from your idols;

---

[1] In the *Westminster Larger Catechism* we are taught that believing and trusting in God, being careful in all things to please him, and sorrowful when in any thing he is offended are among the duties required in the first commandment; and that unbelief, distrust, incorrigibleness, and hardness of heart, or impenitence, (according to Romans 2:5 there quoted) are among the sins forbidden in it.

and turn away your faces from all your abominations' (*Ezek.* 14:6). God 'now commandeth all men every where to repent' (*Acts* 17:30). True repentance then is necessary for it is peremptorily commanded by the Lord. It is a duty from the performance of which no individual can plead an exemption; an exercise which on no account whatever can be dispensed with. All are commanded to repent, and therefore all are bound, in obedience to the Divine command, to exercise true repentance. This high command was often repeated, not only by the ancient prophets and John the Baptist, but by our Lord Jesus himself and his apostles.

2. *True repentance is indispensably requisite because all have sinned.*

All men are sinners, and therefore all need repentance. A sinner cannot be saved from the love, power, and practice of sin in any other way than by being enabled to repent of sin. He cannot serve the Lord acceptably, except he turn from all iniquity to him. Nor can he have communion with him but in proportion to the degree of his repentance for having sinned against him. The law as a covenant of works condemns every sinner who is under it; and consequently it can justify no one who has but in a single instance transgressed it. The unnumbered multitude of a sinner's transgressions, though it cannot add to the certainty, yet will add to the greatness of his condemnation, and should therefore add to the depth of his repentance. Could a man be found who had but in a single instance failed to yield perfect obedience, even such a man would need repentance. He could not be saved without it. How necessary then is repentance for that sinner whose iniquities are more in number than the sand on the sea-shore!

3. *To repent of sin is needful, because all the children of Adam have destroyed themselves by sin.*

'O Israel, thou hast destroyed thyself' (*Hos.* 13:9). 'Return unto the Lord thy God; for thou hast fallen by thine iniquity' (*Hos.* 14:1). The dreadful curse of the violated law is denounced against the impenitent sinner. 'The wrath of God abideth on him' (*John* 3:36). Death in all its extent closely pursues him. Everlasting destruction awaits him. His judgment lingereth not, and his damnation slumbereth not (2 *Pet.* 2:3). That great and terrible God, whom he has times and ways without number insulted, is at once the witness, the judge, and the avenger of all his crimes. The sinner cannot hide so much as one of his transgressions from God's omniscient eye. He cannot resist his infinite power, nor endure his fiery indignation. Can his hands be strong, or can his heart endure when this most tremendous sentence shall sound in his ears: 'Depart from me, ye cursed, into everlasting fire, prepared for the devil and his angels' (*Matt.* 25:41)? These are the words of him who hath said, 'Heaven and earth shall pass away, but my words shall not pass away' (*Matt.* 24:35). Now except the sinner repent, he shall inevitably and eternally perish under the endless execution of that unspeakably dreadful sentence. After his hard and impenitent heart he treasures up unto himself wrath against the day of wrath (*Rom.* 2:5). Ah! secure sinner, you have departed far from the Lord; your soul is pledged that you will return to him by repentance. But if you return not, your precious pledge is lost — irrecoverably lost. The all-important matter is brought to this point — Repent, or perish for ever. How shall you be able to grapple through all eternity with almighty vengeance, with the overwhelming wrath, not only of God, but of the Lamb? (*Isa.* 33:14). This gracious and compassionate call is now addressed to you, 'Repent, and turn from all your transgressions; so iniquity shall not be your ruin' (*Ezek.* 18:30).

4. *True repentance is necessary because God has pledged his faithfulness, that he will execute the tremendous sentence of his violated law upon all who live and die impenitent.*

'Except ye repent', says the Lord Jesus, 'ye shall all perish' (*Luke* 13:3). Without evangelical repentance, salvation is impossible; damnation is inevitable. 'God is angry with the wicked every day. If he turn not, he will whet his sword; he hath bent his bow and made it ready' (*Psa.* 7:11-12; 9:17). 'Hath he said and shall he not do it? or hath he spoken, and shall he not make it good?' (Num. 23:19). If the sinner then do not turn from his sins by sincere repentance, God has pledged his faithfulness that he shall perish. Either his iniquities or his soul must go. To turn to the Lord or to burn in the fire of his fierce indignation are the awful alternatives. Happy should the impenitent sinner be if his transgressions would part from him at the grave, but they shall lie down with him in the dust (*Job* 20:11). Happy would he be if they should lie down with him there and never rise again. But God has said that he 'shall bring every work into judgment, with every secret thing' (*Eccles.* 12:14). Nothing can be hid from the omniscient judge. Nor is he capable of forgetting the least insult that the impenitent sinner ever offered to his glorious majesty. As God is true and cannot lie, the finally impenitent sinner shall spend all eternity, in 'the lake which burneth with fire and brimstone' (*Rev.* 21:8). 'The smoke of his torment, shall ascend up for ever and ever' (*Rev.* 14:11). If there is any meaning in words, if any idea of eternal torments can be conveyed by human language, then the wicked 'shall go away into everlasting punishment' (*Matt.* 25:26). 'Consider this, ye that forget God, lest he tear you in pieces, and there be none to deliver' (*Psa.* 50:22).

5. *To repent of sin is indispensably requisite because God's determination to execute upon impenitent sinners the awful sentence of his violated law is highly just and reasonable.*

Every sin, because it is committed against the infinite majesty of heaven, is objectively an infinite evil. But an infinite moral evil justly deserves an infinite natural evil, or in other words, an infinite punishment. And as a finite creature is incapable of suffering an infinite punishment, except in an infinite, or which is the same, an eternal duration, it is just, it is reasonable that the punishment of the finally impenitent should be eternal. God's resolution then to execute this most dreadful punishment upon such a sinner is most equitable and reasonable. Besides, every sinner who persists in impenitence excuses himself, and by excusing himself, he condemns God. 'Wilt thou', said the Lord to Job, 'disannul my judgment? Wilt thou condemn me, that thou mayest be righteous?' (*Job* 40:8). Why does the sinner transgress the law of God, if he does not account it too strict? Does he say that he has not transgressed it deliberately, but only through inadvertence? Then why does he not repent? His vindication of his continuance in sin implies at once an unjust censure of the law of God, as incompatible with his happiness, and an injurious censure of the justice of God in condemning sinners to eternal punishment. Now, should the Lord save the sinner who thus persists in condemning him, he would seem to plead guilty to the charge. Every hope which a sinner cherishes of salvation in impenitence proceeds on the blasphemous supposition that God, in order to favour an impenitent rebel, will consent to his own dishonour. Except a sinner then in the exercise of true repentance be disposed from his heart to say with Daniel, 'O Lord, righteousness belongeth unto thee; but unto us confusion of faces . . . because we have sinned against thee' (*Dan.* 9:7-8), he must become a sacrifice to the injured honour of the law and the justice of God. Nothing can be more equitable, nothing more reasonable.

6. *True repentance is needful as an evidence of saving and justifying faith in the heart.*

The exercise of evangelical repentance is one of the fruits, and therefore one of the evidences, of that faith which purifies the heart, and works by love. Although the principle of faith and the principle of repentance are in the moment of regeneration implanted in the soul together and at once, yet the exercise of faith in the order of nature, goes before the exercise of true repentance. 'They shall look upon me whom they have pierced, and they shall mourn for him' (*Zech.* 12:10). It is true, none begins to exercise saving faith, but a penitent sinner; that is, one who has the principle of true repentance, as well as that of saving faith, in his heart. Still, however, the exercise of faith, which is a cordial trust in redeeming mercy, precedes the exercise of that repentance which is spiritual and acceptable to God through Jesus Christ. The latter is one of the native fruits and evidences of the former; and therefore it is necessary as such. The exercise of true repentance always follows the acting of true faith.

7. *Evangelical repentance is necessary also as a means of attaining a comfortable sense of judicial pardon of sin, and as an evidence of having received it.*

Saving faith, from which all true repentance proceeds, completes in its first exercise our union with Christ, in whom we cannot but be justified. Although the first exercise of true repentance, then, is not in order of nature prior to the pardon of sin in justification, yet that exercise is indispensably requisite to the comfortable sense of this pardon. It is necessary also as an evidence of a man's having received this forgiveness of sin. If he is not exercising evangelical repentance, his pretensions to faith and to justification by faith are vain. He can have no true sense, no real intimation of the forgiveness of his sins; nor can he have any sure evidence of his being in a state of justification. 'I will sprinkle clean water upon you, and ye shall be clean: from all your filthiness, and from all your idols, will I cleanse you' (*Ezek.* 36:25). 'That thou mayest remember, and be confounded, and never open thy mouth any more because of thy shame, when I am pacified toward thee for all that thou hast done, saith the Lord GOD' (*Ezek.* 16:63).

8. *The exercise of true repentance is indispensably requisite in order to receive God's paternal pardon, and so to be delivered from his chastisement for sin.*

By paternal pardon is not meant that forgiveness of all sin which forms a part of justification, but that fatherly pardon which consists in a believer's deliverance from the guilt which he is daily contracting, by sinning against God as his God and Father, namely, the guilt which renders him liable to the painful effects of paternal displeasure. Now, the frequent exercise of true repentance, as well as of faith, is necessary to his reception of this pardon; and therefore, it must precede his reception of it. As the believer is, by his sins of infirmity, daily contracting this guilt, so the daily exercise of faith and repentance, is necessary to the daily removal of it. For although faith and repentance do not give the smallest title to deliverance from this guilt; yet the frequent exercise of them is a necessary means of that deliverance. If the true Christian does not exercise them daily, he suffers this guilt to accumulate upon him; which will expose him to some of the dreadful effects of paternal displeasure. Accordingly, the Lord gave this invitation to his ancient people: 'Return, thou backsliding Israel, saith the LORD, and I will not cause mine anger to fall upon you; for I am merciful, saith the Lord, and I will not keep anger for ever. Only acknowledge thine iniquity, that thou hast transgressed against the LORD thy God' (*Jer.* 3:12-13). The apostle John also says, 'If we confess our sins, he is faithful and just to forgive us our sins, and to cleanse us from all unrighteousness' (*1 John* 1:9).

9. *The exercise of true repentance is necessary, in token of gratitude for the spiritual blessings and temporal good things bestowed on believers.*

All blessings whether spiritual or temporal, have been forfeited by sin, and yet the Lord daily loads his people with benefits. These mercies and the gracious manner of conferring them, are strong ties and powerful inducements to the daily exercise of evangelical repentance. 'Despisest thou', says the apostle, 'the riches of his goodness and forbearance and longsuffering; not knowing that the goodness of God leadeth thee to repentance?' (*Rom.* 2:4). The multiplied favours which God vouchsafes to the unregenerate, and those especially which he daily confers on believers, tend to melt their hearts into ingenuous sorrow and contrition for their innumerable sins against him, and by his grace to constrain them, to turn to love and obedience. All true believers are grateful to the Lord for the gifts of his bounty, and above all, for the blessings of his grace; and in proportion as they are so, they are impelled to the exercise of that repentance which arises from faith working by love.

10. *Such repentance is indispensably requisite for it is an essential part of that great salvation, which the Lord Jesus has bought and dispenses to his people.*

Instead of being a condition upon which salvation is suspended it is a part of salvation; of that whole salvation, which is bestowed as an absolutely free gift on sinners infinitely unworthy of it. It is an essential ingredient in that everlasting salvation with which Israel shall be saved in the Lord Jesus; and at the same time an appointed means of bringing that salvation to perfection. It is a necessary part of true holiness in its commencement and progress in the soul, and a necessary mean of attaining its consummation. Hence it is called 'repentance to salvation not to be repented of' (*2 Cor.* 7:10), and 'repentance unto life' (*Acts* 11:18). Without it as a part of salvation from the power and practice of sin, or as a branch of evangelical holiness, no man shall see the Lord (*Heb.* 12:14). According to the *Westminster Larger Catechism* it is included in sanctification (Question 75). Indeed it is absolutely impossible for adult persons ever to die to sin in sanctification without a true sense of sin, godly sorrow for it, hatred of it, and self-loathing because of it. Equally impossible is it for them to live to righteousness otherwise than by turning sincerely from the love and practice of all iniquity to the love and practice of universal holiness. Without the exercise of true repentance, then, a man can have no sure evidence, either of regeneration or of sanctification. All who are sanctified exercise evangelical repentance daily in proportion to the degree of their sanctification. And they exercise it, not that it may give them the smallest title to salvation, but that, being itself a part of salvation, it may be an evidence to their consciences that their salvation is begun and gradually advancing. So much for the necessity of evangelical repentance.

***

From what has now been stated it is plain that impenitence under the gospel is absolutely inexcusable. It cannot admit the smallest shadow of excuse. If the works of creation and the dispensations of providence to mankind in general are sufficient to leave the very heathens without excuse (Rom. 1:20), how much more shall the calls and warnings, not only of creation and providence, but of the express Word of God render sinners who hear the gospel inexcusable if they repent not! Sinner, whatever expedients you may employ for preserving the life of your lusts, and for keeping yourself from the unpleasant exercise of repentance, they will be but fig-leaf coverings before the omniscient and righteous Judge of the world. If you say, 'I am not able to repent', this will be no excuse; for true repentance is a part of salvation, offered and promised in the gospel, and the offer and promise are directed to you (*1 John* 5:11; *Prov.* 1:23; *Acts* 2:38-39). If you say, 'I cannot believe those offers and promises with application to myself', neither will this be accepted as an excuse, for the offer and promise of faith to believe them are also addressed to you (*Rev.* 22:17; *Matt.* 12:21; *Heb.* 4:1). Trust in Christ Jesus then, upon the ground of the offer, for the grace of true repentance; and in the faith of the promise, attempt frequently the exercise of it.

Does my reader say, 'I see, at least in my own case, no need of repentance?' Ah! you seem to be one of that generation 'that are pure in their own eyes, and yet is not washed from their filthiness' (*Prov.* 30:12). You deny your crimes, instead of bewailing and confessing them, saying, 'I have done no wickedness' (*Prov.* 30:20). If you had but once, and that in the smallest instance, failed to yield perfect obedience to the holy law of God you could not but need repentance. It would be your duty, and without it your salvation would be impossible. How needful then must repentance be for you whose iniquities are in number more than the hairs of your head!

I do not imagine that it is only those whose abominations are exposed to every eye that need repentance. It may be you have been restrained from doing things which are accounted base in the sight of men; and possibly, you so overrate the external regularity of your conduct as to suppose that you have no cause for godly sorrow or self-loathing, and that you are injured much by being called to the exercise of true repentance. Or perhaps self-pleasing thoughts of your own supposed rectitude hold such firm possession of your mind that you cannot believe it to be proper for one of your fair character to feel shame and sorrow for his sins, or to seek for such a change of heart as is requisite to the exercise of true repentance. But consider, I intreat you, that a charge of great and aggravated disobedience stands in full force against you. The Scripture has concluded all under sin, and you in particular. True repentance, therefore, is as needful for you as if your iniquities were open and glaring. It is as necessary for you as it was for the self-righteous Pharisee in the parable (*Luke* 18:11-12). You are a sinner, and therefore, except you repent, you shall perish. The sinner who lives and dies impenitent shall surely be punished with everlasting destruction. Though signal judgments of a temporal nature do not pursue every impenitent sinner, yet eternal punishment will. Let him be who he will, if he is a sinner, he must either repent or perish. Be he a greater or a lesser sinner, he must be a penitent sinner, else it had been good for him if he had never been born. Either his sin or his soul must yield. Either he must turn from all iniquity or burn through all eternity in the fire of God's fierce indignation. He has it from the mouth of the Saviour himself, in most plain and peremptory terms that except he repent, he shall perish (*Luke* 13:3, 5). Heaven and earth shall pass away, but his words shall not pass away. The finally impenitent sinner, then, shall certainly continue through all eternity in the lake that burns with fire and brimstone.

The Lord has established as sure a connection between true repentance and life eternal, as between impenitence and eternal death. This is his gracious invitation to sinners, 'Repent, and turn from all your transgressions; so iniquity shall not be your ruin' (*Ezek.* 18:30). All denunciations of Divine wrath are summonses to repent; and they have always this clause implied in them, 'Except ye repent.' It is not falling occasionally into sins of infirmity, but continuing impenitent in sin, that ruins multitudes to whom the gospel is preached (*John* 3:19). God in Christ is now on a throne of mercy. He stretches out his golden sceptre of peace and invites the chief of sinners to come near and touch it. And should not the revelation of mercy, and the offer of an indemnity, touch the heart of rebels and constrain them to relent? Should not bowels of mercy, and offers of pardon draw them? If they cordially believe, and by faith receive out of the fullness of Christ the grace of evangelical repentance, they shall certainly be saved. No true penitents shall go to hell. Heaven will be the place of their eternal abode. They who turn from all their iniquities, and return to God now, shall for ever be with him in his holy place on high.

Are all unregenerate sinners commanded to repent? It is then the law as a covenant of works, or as the law of creation, under which they are, that requires true repentance from them. It is true that the law in its federal form knows no place for repentance and makes no provision for exercising it acceptably. It contains no promise of strength with which it may be exercised. But as, supposing the revelation and offer of a Saviour in the gospel, the law as a covenant obliges sinners to believe in him; so, supposing the descendants of Adam to have sinned, the same law obliges them to repent or turn to the Lord.[2] The law as a covenant indeed does not expressly and absolutely call for true repentance; yet hypothetically and virtually it calls for it. It commands all unregenerate sinners to repent; and as a rule of duty, it enjoins all true believers to renew the exercise of repentance. The repentance of a believer is called evangelical repentance because it flows from faith in Jesus Christ as offered in the gospel, and because it is exercised under the influence of the covenant of grace, and according to the law as a rule of life.

What has been stated requires me to exhort the unregenerate sinner speedily to repent. You have sinned against the Lord, times and ways innumerable. O repent then, and turn from all your iniquities to him. Repent without delay. Today, whilst you hear his voice, harden not your heart. Persist no longer, go on no further in your impenitence. One step more may set you beyond a probability of ever returning to the Lord (*Luke* 14:24). If you delay but an hour longer, the great and terrible

---

[2] It requires them to repent or return to God; but not to seek life by their repentance.

God whom you presume to insult by your continuance in sin may lay you under judicial strokes, and swear in his wrath that you shall never enter into his rest (*Prov.* 29:1). If you put God off today, he may put you off tomorrow. God has promised everlasting salvation to the penitent; but he has not promised so much as tomorrow to the negligent. If you fail to improve the present hour of grace, he may refuse to favour you with another. If you turn off his hand of mercy today, his hand of avenging justice may seize you before tomorrow. You have no absolute certainty of enjoying even the shortest time to come. Consider, O secure sinner, that your innumerable provocations must be viewed, either with tears of penitential sorrow, or in endless torments. If you have committed but a single sin, and die without evangelical repentance, your precious soul is lost for ever. O attempt, before it be too late, the exercise of true repentance. Attempt it in the way of trusting in the Lord Jesus for righteousness and strength. Look unto him, and be saved from your inability to repent.

To enforce this exhortation, consider seriously what sin is, and what punishment it deserves. Consider also the command of God, which obliges you, and his multiplied mercies bestowed on you, which bind you in point of gratitude to repent. Remember that you must die, you know not how soon. Your death is certain, and true repentance is necessary that you may die well. Consider the judgment seat of Christ, before which you must appear. There your state for eternity shall be determined according to your deeds done in the body. Knowing then the terror of the Lord, be persuaded to repent. 'God shall bring every work into judgment, with every secret thing, whether it be good, or whether it be evil' (*Eccles.* 12:14). Your aggravated sins may drop out of your memory, but none of them can be erased from the book of God's remembrance (*Hos.* 13:12). Think on the wrong which you have done to God by your great transgressions. You have wronged him by acting in opposition to his nature and his will, by despising his dear Son, by grieving his Holy Spirit, and by trampling on the Divine authority of his holy law.

Consider seriously the dreadful sufferings of the Lamb of God, and see how loudly they call upon you to repent. How tremendous must be that indignation of God against sin, which is written with the blood of his dear Son shed for the remission of the sins of many! Will you continue any longer in sin, when such dreadful indignation against it appears? How terrible did sin appear on Calvary, where the inexorable justice of God seized and pierced his dearly beloved Son with the sword of infinite vengeance! There our adorable Surety was set up as a mark for the arrows of Divine indignation. Amazing spectacle! The infinite darling of the Father enduring the awful fierceness of his infinite wrath! Do you ask, What was the cause of this? It was the iniquities of the elect imputed to him. O will you not then abhor and forsake sin? When the Lord Jesus, was enduring the infinite punishment due for sin, the earth quaked, the rocks rent, the graves were opened, and the sun was darkened; and will you remain unmoved, and impenitent? Behold, how he loved you! He so loved you as with infinite willingness to lay down his life for you. And will you not so love him, as to hate and bewail, and forsake your sins for him? O pray that his great love in dying for you may constrain you to die to sin.

Is true repentance so necessary, as has been shown? It is inexpressibly dangerous, then, to delay it even for a moment. To delay repentance is infinitely perilous; for the present moment may be your last. Your continuance in sin is a re-acting of all your former crimes, with new aggravations. It strengthens the corruption of your nature, hardens your heart, and so renders evangelical repentance the more difficult. It provokes the Lord to deny you grace to repent. During four thousand years, Scripture records but a single instance of true repentance in dying moments. Consider that the longer you continue impenitent, the more is spiritual death advancing upon you. Every sin alienates you more from the life of God, and removes you a step further from him. And in what can this terminate but in eternal separation from him? A state of sin is a state of wrath, in which destruction compasses a man about on every side. 'He that believeth not the Son shall not see life; but the wrath of God abideth on him' (*John* 3:36). To have remained in Sodom on the day in which it was to be consumed would have been dangerous; but to remain a moment longer in the state of wrath is much more perilous. Who would not leave without delay the house that is already on fire? And will you venture to remain another hour in the state of impenitence? Whilst you continue in this inexpressibly dreadful state, there is but a step between you and eternal death. All the security that you have in this condition is but the brittle thread of life, which may be broken by the slightest touch; and then your precious soul shall drop into the place of unutterable and endless torment. 'The wicked shall be turned into hell' (*Psa.* 9:17). The least postponement of true repentance is a risking of eternal happiness or misery on the continuance of a life which may in a moment be taken from you, truly a self-destructive course. It is directly contrary to the calls of the gospel, which are not for tomorrow but for today. 'Today, if ye will hear his voice, harden not your hearts' (*Heb.* 3:7-8). The calls of the gospel to faith and repentance require immediate compliance. They do not allow you time to deliberate whether you will believe and repent or not. To delay compliance is to refuse it; and to refuse it is inexpressibly dangerous. 'Behold, now is the accepted time; behold, now is the day of salvation' (2 *Cor.* 3:2).

How lamentable is the condition of that sinner who delays true repentance! Ah! sinner, you are under a spiritual distemper of the most inveterate kind, and are in imminent danger of eternal death. The compassionate Physician comes to you, offers you an effectual remedy, and intreats you to receive it. You do not peremptorily refuse; but you delay. In the meantime your disease is increasing, and eternal death is advancing with sure steps. 'Your judgment lingereth not, and your damnation slumbereth not' (2 *Pet.* 2:3). Yet you still delay. Ah, deep infatuation! Ah, destructive madness! Tears of blood are not sufficient to bewail it. Poor slothful sinner! You do not consider the amiable excellence of Christ, the value of your immortal soul, the worth of precious time, the weight of infinite and endless wrath, nor how very near your destruction may be. Destruction is ready at your side. You are exposed to the most dreadful surprise. And oh, how horrible, how overwhelming must it be to be past hope, before you begin to fear never to awake from your sinful security till you begin to lift up your despairing eyes in torment! Alas! you do not consider how utterly unable you are to ward off the impending, the fatal blow. Can you, a worm of the dust, stand before the omnipotent Jehovah, whose vengeance is intolerable, whose indignation will burn to the lowest hell, and whose patience may wear out, ere you awake from your lethargy? 'Can thine heart endure, or can thine hands be strong, in the days that I shall deal with thee? I the LORD have spoken it, and will do it' (*Ezek.* 22:14). Ah! you do not consider that if patience retire from the field, avenging justice will succeed in its room; and then, your security shall issue in unutterable and eternal torment. Ah! the folly, the sinfulness, the danger, of delaying repentance toward God!

What has been said, respecting the necessity of evangelical repentance administers reproof to those believers who suffer themselves on any pretence to delay the renewed exercise of it. As spiritual sloth remains in a great measure in believers, so it is productive of delays. When their graces are not in exercise, and communion with God in their duties is not enjoyed, sloth so prevails in them as to make them put off from time to time, the direct exercise of faith and repentance (*Song of Sol.* 5:2-3). Often do they resolve to try the state of their souls and to search what evidences of union with Christ they have, but still the sluggish heart draws back and the solemn trial is delayed. Sometimes the believer delays resolutely to forsake some secret idol that mars his communion with God. Again and again he resolves to renounce and mortify it, but he delays from one time to another to execute his purpose (*Psa.* 66:18). And thus he suffers it to lie as a corroding worm at the root of his fruitfulness and comfort. He delays also some particular duty which he is persuaded the Lord calls him to perform. He often resolves to attempt it, but still one thing or another interposes, and the performance of it is put off till a more convenient time.

In a word, he is convinced that it is far from being an easy thing to die well. He resolves therefore through grace to labour to attain actual preparation for that solemn event. But like the foolish virgins, who, while the bridegroom tarried, all slumbered and slept (*Matt.* 25:5), he delays till some future opportunity the all-important work. Now to such a dilatory Christian I must say, 'What meanest thou, O sleeper? arise, call upon thy God, if so be that God will think upon you that you perish not' (*Jon.* 1:6). The longer you delay, do you not find yourself the farther from your purpose? Does not your backwardness to spiritual exercise increase upon you the more? Is not that the way to come to poverty? Shall not the idle soul suffer hunger? Have not you sometimes awaked like Samson, and found your spiritual strength gone when you had most occasion for it? May not opportunities of doing good soon be taken from you, or you from them? And will not the work of actual preparation for death be the harder, the longer it is delayed? When death is approaching, you shall have less ability, greater opposition, and yet more work to do, than otherwise you should have. Are not you then much to be blamed for deferring any of your duties, and especially the frequent exercise of faith and repentance?

It administers reproof also to the unregenerate sinner who delays repentance. How much are you, O secure sinner, to be blamed for deferring work so necessary as that of repentance to salvation! You are under the dreadful curse of the violated law. The wrath of that great and terrible God, whom you have times without number insulted, abides on you. The wrath to come is ready to seize and overwhelm you and yet you delay repentance. You continue still in the love and practice of sin. 'How long wilt thou sleep, O sluggard? when wilt thou arise out of thy sleep?' Your answer apparently will be, 'Yet a little sleep, a little slumber, a little folding of the hands to sleep' (*Prov.* 6:9-10). But why do you sleep securely in impenitence, when you know not what a day may bring forth? Why do you not begin without the least delay to prepare by true repentance for happy eternity?

It may be you resolve to repent when you shall have more leisure than now, or when you shall be old. But how can you be certain that you shall attain old age? Is it not as likely that the Lord, whose wrath you are continuing to provoke, may say, 'Thou fool, this night thy soul shall be required of thee' (*Luke* 12:20)? The time of your life is but as a day—a short day—and you have much work to do. A great part of your day is past already; and will you sleep on, till the night come when no man can work? Will you thus risk the salvation of your immortal soul upon an absolute uncertainty? Is it old age, the very dregs of your time, that you resolve to devote to God? But ah! what certainty can you have that an infinitely holy God will accept these at your hand? 'If ye offer the blind for sacrifice, is it not evil? and if ye offer the lame and sick, is it not evil? Offer it now unto thy governor; will he be pleased with thee, or accept thy person? saith the LORD of hosts' (*Mal.* 1:8). Suppose you should be spared till you become old; there are few, very few, who get grace to repent acceptably when they grow old. Some indeed, as is represented in one of our Lord's parables, were called effectually at the eleventh hour (*Matt.* 20:6). But these were not the same persons that were standing idle either at the third, or sixth, or ninth hour. Be not emboldened then to delay true repentance, because some were called at the eleventh hour.

If men, from their earliest years, live under a pure dispensation of the gospel, and yet spend their best days in the love and service of sin, it is God's usual way to leave them, when they are old, under blindness of mind and hardness of heart. 'His bones are full of the sin of his youth, which shall lie down with him in the dust' (*Job* 20:11). The Lord may, indeed, in the case of a few individuals, depart from the usual tenor of his procedure. But ah! it is a desperate adventure for a sinner to presume upon this. I intreat you, then, to trust without delay in the great Redeemer for grace to repent; and in the faith of pardoning mercy, as well as of renovating grace, resolutely to attempt the exercise of it. O delay it not a moment longer, lest you sleep the sleep of death, of eternal death. 'Evil pursueth sinners' (*Prov.* 13:21). If it overtake you in unbelief and impenitence, the smoke of your torment shall ascend up for ever and ever (*Rev.* 14:11). The Father of mercies, the God of all grace, who hath spared you till now, with infinite compassion still invites you; and the Lord Jesus stands with open arms ready to embrace you. he complains that you will not come to him, that you may have life; affirms with an oath, that he hath no pleasure in the death of a sinner; and with the tenderest compassion adds, 'Turn ye, turn ye, why will ye die?' (*Ezek.* 33:11). O! do not disregard such admonitions, such compassions, such invitations, such expostulations; but upon the warrant of the gospel offer, trust in the Lord Jesus for that repentance to salvation, and that forgiveness of sins, which he is exalted to give to all who cordially trust in him (*Acts* 5:32).

The following directions how to attain evangelical repentance I would now offer to the impenitent sinner.

1. *Look upon it as the gift of Christ, and trust that your iniquities were laid on him, and that he was pierced for them* (Zech. 12:10).

Trust also in him for true repentance, and in God through him, for pardoning mercy and renewing grace. You should attempt believing, in order to the exercise of evangelical repentance, and should rely on the grace of God in Christ for the renovating influences of his Holy Spirit.

2. *Choose God in Christ for your covenant-God and portion, and then you will be both disposed and encouraged to return to him.*

To return to God as the Lord your God is the essence of evangelical repentance.

3. *Be frequent and importunate in prayer to him for the gift of true repentance, saying with Ephraim, 'Turn thou me, and I shall be turned; for thou art the* LORD *my God'* (Jer. 31:18).

Pray in faith for the performance of this absolute promise to you: 'A new heart will I give you, and a new spirit will I put within you; and I will take away the stony heart out of your flesh, and I will give you an heart of flesh' (*Ezek.* 36:26).

4. *Endeavour to see sin in its own hateful colours, to see what an evil and bitter thing it is* (Jer. 2:19).

To see the sin of your heart and life in its exceeding

sinfulness and odiousness would be a means of making you flee from it with deep abhorrence. And if you would discern spiritually the hateful deformity of sin, consider the infinite majesty and holiness of God which are insulted by sin, the good things which impenitent continuance in sin deprives you of, the dreadful evils to which it exposes you, the infinite wrath of God which awaits you if you live and die impenitent, and the infinite obligation under which you lie to keep all his commandments.

5. *Study to see and to be suitably affected with the deep depravity or sin of your nature, as well as with the innumerable transgressions of your life; and call yourself every day to a strict account for your sins of omission and commission on that day; and that, in order to see what great reason you have to repent of them.*

6. *Meditate frequently and attentively on the awful anguish, and astonishing death of the Lord Jesus, that you may see the exceeding sinfulness of sin, and the everlasting punishment which the sinner deserves.*

7. *Dwell much on the thoughts of death and of judgment to come.*

Consider seriously how uncertain is the continuance of your life in this world. Be assured that if death surprise you in unbelief and impenitence, you are for ever undone. Think also of the awful tribunal of that righteous and inexorable Judge, whose eyes are as a flame of fire, before which you must appear; where every finally impenitent sinner shall, according to the demerits of his deeds done in the body, be sentenced to everlasting punishment. O! how tremendous, how overwhelming will be the sentence pronounced on the impenitent: 'Depart from me, ye cursed, into everlasting fire, prepared for the devil and his angels' (*Matt.* 25:41). O consider this, and by faith and repentance flee speedily from the wrath to come.

4: THE DIFFERENCE BETWEEN TRUE AND COUNTERFEIT REPENTANCE

It is a truth clearly revealed and often inculcated in Scripture that without repentance a man cannot attain eternal life in heaven. The most of men, therefore, who read and hear the gospel admit that repentance is necessary to their future safety and felicity. But while they believe that it cannot be well with them except they repent, they resolve with a fatal precipitance to call something by this name which bears only a faint resemblance to it; and then they flatter themselves that this base counterfeit will not only be acceptable to God but will even recommend them to his favour. Persuading themselves that they have already repented, they compose themselves to sleep on the pillow of carnal security; and they will not believe that any of the dreadful threatenings denounced in Scripture against impenitent sinners belongs to them. Thus many 'go down to the grave with a lie in their right hand.' They obstinately refuse to be convinced of their fatal mistake till they begin to lift up their despairing eyes in torment. That my reader may not through ignorance deceive himself with a repentance which must be repented of, I shall endeavour to show him the difference between a true and a counterfeit repentance, as distinctly and plainly as I can, under the following particulars:

1. *False repentance flows from a counterfeit faith of the law as a covenant of works; but true repentance follows a true faith both of the law and of the gospel.*

False repentance arises from a counterfeit faith of the violated law in its covenant form. Hence it is often styled legal repentance, and the conviction of sin which excites it, legal conviction. It flows from that temporary faith of the commands and curses of the broken law, which a legalist, when his conscience is at any time alarmed, reluctantly exercises. When the holy law strikes his conscience, he is forced to believe that it requires from him perfect obedience as the condition of life, and that its tremendous curse for innumerable instances of disobedience is pronounced against him (*Gal.* 3:10). The righteous law claims perfect obedience as due from him and condemns him for his disobedience. His awakened conscience concurs with the precept and curse of the law, so that he begins to be greatly alarmed. The only refuge from the curse of the law to which he has recourse in order to pacify his guilty conscience, to satisfy Divine justice, and to lay a foundation of hope, is resolutions, reformations, duties, and other self-righteous schemes. The defects of his endeavours and attainments create new fears; these fears excite new endeavours; and thus the legal penitent goes on, without attaining to the law of righteousness, because he 'seeks it not by faith, but as it were by the works of the law' (*Rom.* 9:31-32). As he may at the same time have a temporary faith of the gospel, he may pretend some regard to Christ in this his legal progress. He may hope that God, for the sake of Christ, will accept his repentance and forgive his sins. And what is this but a secret hope that the redemption of Jesus Christ will impart such merit to his tears, reformations, and works, as will make them effectual to atone for his sins, and to purchase the favour of God? He cannot trust that God will show mercy to him, till, by his penitence and reformation, he recommend himself to his favour.

On the other hand, the characters of true repentance are directly opposite to those now mentioned. It follows a sincere, a spiritual faith, both of the law and of the gospel. Whilst a true conviction of sin and misery flows from a spiritual belief of the law with application to oneself, a true sense of sin, from which genuine repentance springs, arises from a sincere faith, both of the law and of the gospel. It is the immediate consequence of a sincere faith of pardoning mercy. 'There is forgiveness with thee', says the Psalmist, 'that thou mayest be feared' (*Psa.* 130:4). Godly sorrow for sin, and turning from the love and practice of sin to the love and practice of holiness, flow, as was stated above, from reliance on the righteousness of Jesus Christ for all our title to pardon and sanctification, and from trusting in him for pardoning mercy and sanctifying grace. Hence it is called evangelical repentance. The acting of true faith produces, in order of nature, the exercise of this repentance. He who would repent acceptably must first believe in Christ that he may so repent (*Heb.* 11:6; *Acts* 11:21). He must believe that there is safety in entrusting his guilty soul to Christ before he can, with sincerity and good courage, turn from all sin to God in him. He must be united to Christ by faith, as the branch to the vine, before he can bring forth such fruit as is meet for repentance. Accordingly, the true penitent approaches to a gracious God with deep convictions of his guilt and of his desert of eternal rejection from him; but then, he comes before a mercy-seat. He relies on the blood of Jesus Christ for purification from his innumerable sins; and from that he takes encouragement to mourn before the Lord, and to express himself in the language of the royal penitent, 'Wash me throughly from mine iniquity, and cleanse me from my sin.' 'Create in me a clean heart, O God, and renew a right spirit within me' (*Psa.* 51:2, 10). That is the prospect which both encourages and invigorates his humble supplications for mercy and grace. That is it which embitters all his sins to him, which makes him loathe them and long earnestly for complete deliverance from the love and practice of them.

Here, the attentive reader cannot but discern the difference, nay contrariety, between a guilty flight from God, like that of Adam after his fall, and a humbling, self-condemning approach to his pardoning mercy, like that of the prodigal when returning to his father's house; between slavish and proud endeavours to atone for our sins, and to make our peace with God by our own righteousness, and resorting solely to the blood of Christ for cleansing from all sin. Similarly he sees the difference between mourning for our own danger by sin, and mourning for our sins themselves as the basest injuries done to God and Christ, and to the mercy and love which were displayed to us in Christ. And again, he sees the difference between attempting a new life by the strength of our own resolutions and endeavours, and trusting only in the mercy of the Lord Jesus for sanctifying as well as for justifying grace.

2. *Counterfeit repentance proceeds only from a sense of danger and a dread of wrath; but true repentance is a sincere mourning for sin, a loathing of ourselves in our own sight for it, and an earnest desire of deliverance from the power and practice of it.*

In false repentance the sinner is most affected with the dreadful consequences of his transgression (*Isa.* 59:9-12); but in evangelical or true repentance the believer is chiefly affected with the malignity and odiousness of sin itself as contrary to the holy nature and law of God (*Luke* 15:21).

In false repentance the conscience of the sinner is alarmed by a sense of his dreadful guilt and danger; and then it cannot but remonstrate loudly against those sins which threaten him with intolerable and eternal torment. Hence those terrors which are frequently found among awakened sinners under apprehensions of approaching death. At such times their innumerable sins stare them in the face, and their high aggravations are remembered with bitter remorse. Conscience draws up the indictment and brings home the charge against them. The violated law condemns them without mercy. And what have they now in prospect? What but a certain fearful looking for of judgment and fiery indignation to devour them? Now, with what deep distress will they cry out and howl upon their beds because of the heinousness and demerit of their sins! With what amazement will they expect the tremendous outcome of their sinful course! How ready will they now be to make resolutions of beginning a humble, a circumspect, a holy life! Under this their terror, conscience like a flaming sword keeps them from their former course of impiety and sensuality.

And what is all this repentance, but the fear of the worm that never dies, and of the fire that shall never be quenched? Let conscience but be pacified, and the tempest of the troubled mind allayed, and these false penitents will return with the dog to his vomit (2 *Pet.* 2:22), until some new alarm revive their convictions of sin and danger, and with them, the same process of repentance. Thus many sin and repent, and repent and sin, all their lives. Or it may be, distress of conscience makes a deeper impression, and fixes such an abiding dread of some particular sins that a visible reformation appears. Yet in this case the sinner's lusts are only dammed up by his fears, and were the dam but broken down, they would immediately run again in their former channel with increasing force. It is true, this legal terror is, in many of the elect, a preparative to evangelical repentance. Many true penitents were, sometime, in the same distressing circumstances and at first began from no better principle than self-love to flee from the wrath to come.

It was said that false repentance proceeds only from a sense of danger and a dread of impending wrath. The character of true repentance is the very reverse. Sin itself becomes the heaviest burden, and the object of the greatest abhorrence and dread, to the sincere penitent. As evangelical repentance flows from the faith of pardoning mercy, the fear of hell, though it may sometimes accompany godly sorrow for sin, yet forms no part of this repentance. Godly sorrow springs from an affecting and humbling sense of the dishonour and injury which the true penitent sees he has done to a gracious God by his transgression in the first Adam, by the sin of his nature, and the innumerable evils of his life. This is the grievance, this the distress, of every true penitent. His language runs like this: — 'I acknowledge my transgressions and my sin is ever before me.' 'Mine iniquities are gone over mine head; as an heavy burden, they are too heavy for me.' 'Deliver me from all my transgressions.' 'Let not any iniquity have dominion over me.' 'Innumerable evils have compassed me about; mine iniquities have taken hold upon me, so that I am not able to look up: they are more than the hairs of mine head; therefore my heart faileth me. Be pleased, O LORD, to deliver me: O LORD, make haste to help me' (*Psa.* 51:3; 38:4; 119:133; 40:12-13). Here we see that the sincere penitent mourns for and abhors all his lusts, whether of the flesh or of the mind, and longs to be completely delivered from them. He is willing that none should be spared, no, not even a right hand or a right eye.

How great and obvious, then, is the difference between being struck with dread, restrained by terror, or driven from a course of sinning by the lashes of an awakened conscience; between this, I say, and loathing ourselves in our own sight for our iniquities and abominations, and vehemently desiring grace to mortify our corruption that we may be freed from the power of sin! The former is merely the fruit of self-love which urges the soul to flee from danger; the latter is the exercise of a vital principle which separates the soul from sin, and engages the whole man in a persevering opposition to it.

3. *In false penitence the sinner is chiefly affected with his gross and open sins; whereas in true repentance, the believer is more deeply affected with the secret and darling sins which he formerly delighted to commit.*

In counterfeit repentance the sinner is affected chiefly with his gross and open abominations, and with the connection of endless punishment with them. It is the recollection of his gross and scandalous crimes that fills him with remorse and dread; and it is not so much his view of these abominations themselves that fills him with regret and distress, as his prospect of punishment for them both in time and in eternity. It is their connection with present reproach and with future torment that usually fills his mind with the keenest anguish. Such was the repentance of Cain. After his murder of his brother Abel, he said, 'My punishment is greater than I can bear' (*Gen.* 4:13): or rather as in the margin,—'Mine iniquity is greater than that it may be forgiven.' He did not say, My iniquities, the innumerable sins of which I have hitherto been guilty; but, 'my iniquity', the crime of murder only. Such also was the repentance of Judas the traitor. He said to the chief priests and elders, 'I have sinned in that I have betrayed the innocent blood' (*Matt.* 27:4). It was not for his covetousness, hypocrisy, and other innumerable sins that he appeared to feel remorse, but only for his having betrayed the innocent blood. It was for this most atrocious crime, and this only, together with the sure prospect of endless punishment, that he felt such anguish of mind as was insupportable; for 'he went and hanged himself.' Of the same character is the repentance of multitudes at this day.

On the other hand, in true repentance the believer is ordinarily most affected with a spiritual view of his secret evils; the sin of his nature in general, and the unbelief and legal temper of his heart in particular. And of all his actual transgressions, the remembrance of none usually affects him so deeply as that of his own iniquity, his constitution-sin, the sin which in times past most easily beset him, and most frequently enslaved him. He is affected with sorrow and self-loathing for all his actual sins; but it is a spiritual view of this sin that commonly fills him with the deepest abasement and the keenest contrition.

And whilst, with holy abhorrence of all iniquity, he turns from it to God, he sets himself with peculiar vigilance and diligence against this sin (*Psa.* 51:5-7; *Rom.* 7:23-24; *Heb.* 12:1).

4. *Counterfeit penitence has no true connection with the pardon of sin in justification; but true repentance is a necessary consequence of that act of pardon.*

Legal repentance is not connected with the judicial pardon of sin; for it is the repentance of one who is under the curse of the law as a covenant of works, and therefore under the dominion of sin. It is the repentance of a man who is under the condemning sentence of the broken law, which is the strength of sin; and therefore it is far from being spiritually good and acceptable to God. It is the repentance of an unbeliever; and 'without faith it is impossible to please God' (*Heb.* 11:6). In brief, it is the repentance of a man whose sins are not pardoned, and whose person is not accepted as righteous before God in justification. And as acceptance, according to the covenant of grace, must begin at the person, and then go on to his performances, so, that repentance which does not flow from justification is counterfeit: it has nothing in it that is spiritually good and acceptable to God (*Acts* 2:37; *Rom.* 7:8-13).

On the other hand, true repentance is a necessary fruit of pardon and acceptance as righteous in justification; and therefore the exercise of it is spiritually good and acceptable to the Lord. The believer is freely pardoned,

and made accepted in the Beloved (*Eph.* 1:6); and therefore Divine acceptance proceeds from his person to his
exercise of repentance. Because he himself is accepted
as righteous, his repentance is accepted as sincere. It is
a necessary consequence and evidence of God's judicial
pardon of sin in the act of justification; and it is an
appointed mean of the renewed intimations of it, and
also of fatherly pardon, or the removal of paternal chastisement for sin. 'I have blotted out', says Jehovah, 'as a
thick cloud, thy transgressions, and as a cloud, thy sins:
return unto me, for I have redeemed thee' (*Isa.* 44:22).
And again, 'Return, ye backsliding children, and I will
heal your backslidings' (*Jer.* 3:22);—I as a Father will forgive them, and restore your souls. Although the exercise
of evangelical repentance is impossible under legal guilt,
which tends to the destruction of the sinner, and binds
him under the dominion of sin (*1 Cor.* 15:56; *Rom.* 7:6-
8), yet it frequently exists under that guilt which exposes
the believer to God's fatherly anger, which anger implies
love to his person, and tends to his advancement in the
love and practice of holiness (*Jer.* 31:18-20; *Heb.* 12:6-
11; *Rev.* 3:19).

5. *False penitence commonly issues from discouragement
and despondency, but true repentance from encouraging
hope.*

Many legal penitents, indeed, by their external reformation do pacify their alarmed consciences, settle upon
their lees, and cry, Peace, peace to their souls; and so,

their discouragement and repentance both come to an end. But while their anxious concern remains, their desponding fear is the very life of it. Their innumerable and heinous crimes appear dreadful to their alarmed consciences, as they cannot but know that they frequently violate their promises of new and universal obedience. They are therefore afraid that God will never pardon and accept such perfidious rebels as they have been. And though they dare not neglect religious duties, yet they come with horror into the presence of the Lord, as into that of an inexorable judge, an infinite enemy. Thus they have nothing to keep them from sinking into absolute despair but their good resolutions and endeavours, which yet are too defective to be a ground of comfortable hope. Now what is all this but, with base ingratitude, to undervalue the spotless righteousness of Jesus Christ, to limit the boundless grace and mercy of God, and implicitly to deny the truth of the blessed gospel? They flee from the mercy of God our Saviour, while they pretend to flee to it.

On the other hand, though the true penitent has a deeper sense of the atrociousness of his sins, and of the greatness of his guilt, than any false penitent can have, yet he dares not yield to despairing thoughts of redeeming mercy. He is enabled to trust in the mercy of God his Saviour; and his exercise of faith opens the door of hope, and therefore the door of repentance. It is granted that he may labour for a time under many discouraging fears, but these are his infirmity, not his repentance. He exercises a living hope, and that gives life and activity to every other grace, and to repentance in particular.

Here it may be observed that, though a fear and jealousy of one's own sincerity may be consistent with the exercise of true repentance, yet all doubts of the freeness of gospel offers and of the faithfulness of gospel promises, all fears of his not being elected, of his having sinned away the day of grace, or of his having sinned against the Holy Spirit, all apprehensions that his sins are so aggravated, so atrocious, as not to admit of pardoning mercy—these are inconsistent with, and destructive of the exercise of it. The evangelical penitent looks over the highest mountains that are raised before him—the greatness of his transgressions, the plagues of his heart, the temptations of Satan—to infinite mercy. Thither he will fly. In that he will hope, though his case seem ever so dark, and though every thing appear to turn against him. And the more lively his hope is, the more humbled and grieved he is for his iniquities, and the more vigorous his endeavours are after new obedience.

Since true repentance is a hatred of, and a departure from all sin, it must surely be an abhorrence of, and a flight from unbelief and despair, the greatest of all sins. It is not, therefore, sufficient for the true penitent to believe that God is infinitely gracious and merciful, that the righteousness of Christ is infinitely meritorious, that there is forgiveness with God for the worst of sinners, and that Christ with his righteousness and fullness is freely offered in the gospel to sinners in common. He must believe all this with application to himself. And in order to his approaching to God as a Father, in order to his being in love with the ways of God, and to his serving him with cheerfulness and delight, he must likewise trust in the Lord Jesus for his whole salvation. This firm trust in the mercy of God his Saviour is not only requisite in order to the first exercise of true repentance, but the sincere penitent will invariably find, that when he at any time yields to a despondent frame, he is hereby rendered incapable of godly sorrow for sin, of delight in God, and of the spiritual performance of any duty. The sincere penitent should, indeed, be jealous and distrustful of himself, but he must not distrust the compassionate Saviour, nor despond, if he would maintain the exercise of evangelical repentance, or of any other spiritual grace.

The difference, then, between a false and a true repentance is as great as between desponding fear and encouraging hope; as between being affrighted by a sight of our sins from trusting in God, and from serving him with delight, and our being allured by his infinite mercy to seek his face, to expect forgiveness through the blood of his dear Son, and to serve him with the dispositions of children.

6. *Counterfeit repentance springs from enmity to God and to his holy law, but true repentance from love to both.*

The grief and terror which legal penitents often feel arise from dreadful apprehensions of God and of his inflexible justice. They know that they have greatly provoked him.

They are afraid of his infinite wrath, and therefore are eager to obtain a covert from it. Previously it may be, they have had some pleasing apprehensions of God, while they considered him as all mercy, and while, though yet living in their sins, they entertained a hope of pardon. But now that they have alarming apprehensions of his infinite holiness and justice—and because he appears an infinite enemy to them, they are contriving some way to make peace with him; for they are afraid that, if the controversy proceed, it will issue in their eternal destruction. They resolve upon obedience to him from the same motives from which slaves obey their tyrannical masters, even though the rule of their obedience is directly contrary to the inclination of their hearts. Were the penalty of the law taken away, their enmity to it would quickly appear. They would soon again with the same pleasure as formerly, embrace their beloved lusts.

The truth of this assertion is frequently witnessed in those who throw off their convictions and reformations together, and who, notwithstanding their appearance of religion, manifest by their sinful and sensual lives the reigning enmity of their hearts to God and his holy law. They still show themselves to be enemies in their minds by their wicked works (*Col.* 1:21). As for their sorrow on account of their sins, such penitents are very sorry that God hates sin so exceedingly that he is resolved to punish it with the everlasting destruction of the impenitent sinner, and that he is able to execute this purpose, in spite of the strongest opposition. They are also extremely sorry, as was hinted above, that his law is so very strict, and that the punishment threatened for sin is so terribly severe; but they are far from being grieved in heart for the base, the ungrateful part they have acted, by sinning against a gracious God and violating his holy law.

The true penitent, on the contrary, mourns, not because the law is very strict or its penalty very severe; for he esteems the law to be holy, and the commandment to be holy, and just, and good. But he grieves that, though the law is spiritual, yet he is carnal, sold under sin. He mourns that his nature has been so contrary to God, that his practice has been so opposite to his will, and that he makes no better progress in mortifying the deeds of the body of sin, and in regulating his affections by the Word of God. He breathes with the same earnestness after sanctification as after freedom from eternal wrath. He loves God and his holy law; and therefore he does not desire that the law should be bent to his corruptions, but that his heart and life should be fully subjected to the law as the rule of his duty. He longs for nothing so much as redemption from sin, proficiency in faith and holiness, and a life of communion with Christ, and with God in him.

The difference, then, between a false penitent and a true one is very great. The former looks upon God with terror and aversion, but the latter mourns his distance from him, and desires earnestly to be transformed into his likeness. The one still loves his sins in his heart, and mourns that there is a law to condemn, and justice to punish him for them; but the other hates all his iniquities without reserve, and because they are contrary to the holy nature and law of God, he is weary under the burden of them. The obedience of the former is by mere constraint, but the imperfections of the latter are such ground of continual humiliation to him as makes him constantly aspire after higher degrees of faith and holiness. The one finds no inward and abiding complacence in the service of God: the other accounts it his happiness, and takes more pleasure in spiritual obedience than in any thing else. In a word, the repentance of the former arises from enmity to God and to his holy law; but the repentance of the latter flows from faith working by love to God and his law.

7. *False repentance produces only a partial and external reformation, but true repentance is a total change of heart, and a universal turning from sin to God.*

As some particular gross iniquity commonly leads the way to that distress or terror which is the evidence of a legal and false repentance, so a reformation with respect to such sins too frequently wears off the impression, and gives rest to the troubled conscience without any further change; or at least, some darling lust will be retained, some right hand or right eye spared. If the false penitent be deterred from sins of commission, he will still live in the omission or careless performance of known duty; or if he be zealous for the duties respecting the worship of God, he will still live in acts of injustice, strife, and uncharitableness toward men. If he reveals some activity in contending for the truths of the gospel, his heart will still cleave to the world, and he will pursue it as the object of his chief desire and supreme delight. If he make conscience of refraining from every open sin, he yet little regards the sins of his heart, such as silent envy, secret pride, self-righteousness, self-preference, earthly-mindedness, malice, unbelief, or some other secret abominations. Whatever progress he may seem to make in religion, his heart is still estranged from the power of godliness. Like Ephraim, he is as 'a cake not turned' (*Hos.* 7:8), neither dough nor bread; or like Laodicea, lukewarm, 'neither cold nor hot' (Rev. 3:15). His mind is not changed with regard to sin. He does not sincerely grieve that ever he committed it, nor does he really wish it undone. He does not heartily abhor it, nor is he ever willing to be finally divorced from it.

The character of the true penitent is directly the reverse of this. He finds, indeed, as has already been observed, continual occasion to lament the great imperfections of his heart and life; and accordingly he relies for renewed pardon on the righteousness of Christ and on the promises of God. But though he has not already attained, neither is already perfect, yet he presses on towards perfection. He watches and strives against all the corruptions of his heart, and labours after increasing conformity to God, in all holy conversation and godliness.[1] He does not

---

[1] The emperor Sigismund having, in a sore fit of sickness, made fair promises of amendment of life, asked Theodoric, Archbishop of Cologne how he might know whether his repentance was sincere. The Archbishop replied, 'If you are as careful to perform in

renounce one lust and retain another, nor content himself with devotional duties, in the neglect of strict honesty, and unfeigned benevolence; neither can he rest till this is his rejoicing, even the testimony of his conscience, that in simplicity and godly sincerity, not with fleshly wisdom but by the grace of God, he has his conversation in the world. All the actings of his mind, as well as his external conduct, fall under his cognizance and inspection; and his daily exercise and desire are to approve himself to him who knows his thoughts afar off. His reformation extends, not only to the devotion of the church, but to that of his family and his closet; not only to his conversation, but to his tempers and affections, and to the duties of every relation which he sustains among men. His repentance produces heavenly-mindedness, humility, meekness, charity, patience, forgiveness of injuries, and self-denial; and it is accompanied by all the other graces and fruits of the Holy Spirit. And in order to be satisfied as to the truth of his repentance, he examines the motives which prevail with him to turn from sin to God for he knows that the mean motives which rise no higher than himself and his own safety can never denominate him a true penitent.

The difference, then, between a false and a true repentance is exceedingly great. The former is only an external reformation, devoid of all spiritual grace, but the latter is an internal change of the will and affections, as well as of the outward conduct, a change which is accompanied by

---

your health, as you are forward to promise in your sickness, you may safely draw that inference.'

all the graces and fruits of the blessed Spirit. The one aims at so much religion only as will keep the mind easy, and calm the tumults of an awakened conscience: the other aims at a holy, humble, and spiritual walk with God, and rests in no degree of conformity to Christ short of perfection.

8. *Once more, counterfeit repentance is only temporary, and it wears off with those convictions of conscience which have occasioned it; but true repentance is the continued exercise of the sincere believer.*

We have frequent instances of persons who for a while appear under the bitterest remorse for their sins, and yet afterwards wear off all their impressions, and return to the same course of impiety and sensuality which occasioned their distress and terror. They hereby declare to the world that their goodness, like that of Ephraim, was but as a morning cloud, and an early dew, which soon pass away. And beside these, there seem to be some who quiet their consciences, and speak peace to their souls, from their having been in distress and terror on account of their sins, from their reformation from certain gross immoralities, and from their formal course of duties. They have repented, they think, and therefore conclude that they are at peace with God; and they seem to have no great concern about either their former impieties or their present iniquities. They conclude that they are converted, and that their state is good and therefore they are secure and dwell at ease. They often think, and perhaps speak, loftily of their experiences. They are elated with joyful apprehensions of the safety of their state and of the goodness of their heart; but they have no humbling impressions of their sins, and no godly sorrow, either for the depravity of their natures, or the imperfection of their duties, or the multitude of their provocations.

Many, whilst under the stings of an awakened conscience, are driven to maintain a solemn watch over their hearts and their lives, to be afraid of every sin, and to be in appearance very conscientious, serious, and even zealous, in the performance of known duties. By this imaginary progress in religion they gradually wear out their convictions, and get over their legal terrors; and then their apparent watchfulness and tenderness of conscience are forgotten. They attend to their duties in a careless manner, with a trifling and remiss frame of soul, while the great concerns of an eternal world are but little in their thoughts. All their religion is reduced to a lifeless, a cold form. They still maintain the form, but appear quite unconcerned about the power of godliness. Besides, false penitents commonly suffer themselves to be basely overcome by the fear of man. They begin seemingly to repent, but loving the praise of man, and not being able to endure the contempt and reviling of the profane for their professed attachment to Christ, they turn away from the holy commandment. The men with whom they are connected, or to whom they are related, or on whom they depend, must at all hazards be respected and pleased.

Evangelical repentance, on the contrary, is a lasting principle. The true penitent loathes and condemns himself daily. Every day he laments and abhors all the evils which he discovers both in his heart and in his life. He does not forget his former sins, nor become unconcerned about them, as soon as he attains peace of conscience and a joyful hope of his reconciliation to God. But the clearer his evidences of the Divine favour are, the more does he loathe and condemn himself for his iniquities, the more vile in his own sight does he appear, and the more aggravated and odious do his past sins appear to him. The faith and sense of pardoning mercy made Paul appear in his own eyes the chief of sinners. The true penitent continues not only to mourn and to abhor himself for his past abominations, but he always finds new cause for the exercise of repentance. He finds daily so much unbelief, legality, and earthly-mindedness in his heart; so much deadness, formality, and hypocrisy in his duties; and so much prevalence of evil inclinations, vain thoughts, inordinate affections, and of the sin which so easily besets him, that he cannot, while he is in this tabernacle, but groan being burdened (2 *Cor.* 5:4). Repentance, therefore, is the constant exercise of the true Christian as long as he is in this world. He will not leave off repenting till he perfectly leaves off sinning. He carries the exercise of repentance about with him as long as he carries about the body of sin (*Rom.* 7:24). Sin follows him whilst he is fleeing from it; often it overtakes him, and therefore he must often renew his flight. For conscience's sake he will forgo temporal advantages, and break through the ties even of sweetest friendship and of nearest kindred, sooner than be drawn back by either into his former neglect of duty. He will maintain a godly jealousy over all persons and things connected with him, lest any of them prove a hindrance to him in his course of new obedience.

Thus it is manifest that the difference between a false and a true repentance is as great as between the running of water in the paths, after a heavy shower, and the streams flowing continually from a living fountain. A false and legal repentance continues no longer than the legal terrors which occasion it, whereas an evangelical repentance is a continued war against sin, until death sound this enemy's retreat. So much for the difference between a true and a counterfeit repentance.

❦

From what has now been stated, the reader may see the difference between true and counterfeit humiliation. Ahab humbled himself from a sense of the danger and a dread of the consequences of sin; but the sincere penitent is humbled from an affecting sense of the malignity, odiousness, and demerit of sin (*Job* 42:5-6). The former had not a true sense of sin, and therefore, under all his pretended humiliation, the pride of his heart retained its complete dominion over him; whereas the latter has a true sight and feeling of the evil and loathsomeness of sin, and therefore he lies low in the dust before God. As an evidence that the pride of his heart is mortified, he sees, abhors and bitterly bewails it. A slave may stoop for fear of the lash, but it is the disposition of a son to be affected with sorrow and self-abasement for any offence he has given to a kind father. The legal penitent may seem very humble under a sense of the evil which his sin has done to himself, whilst his heart is far from being suitably affected with the injury which it has done to the manifested glory of God. He will be deeply affected under an apprehension of God's terrible wrath, whilst his heart is far from being touched with his love.

If the true penitent does evil he takes the blame to himself, but if he does good he gives the praise to God. 'I laboured more abundantly than they all', says our apostle, 'yet not I, but the grace of God which was with me' (*1 Cor.* 15:10). The false penitent, on the contrary, lays the blame of the evil that he does upon others and takes the praise of the good which he does to himself. He who is truly humbled, conscious that he has no righteousness of his own, flies to the mercy, and submits to the righteousness of Jesus Christ, as the sole ground of his justification. This is that distinguishing character of evangelical humiliation to which the legal penitent cannot produce the smallest claim. The former is made willing to receive the whole of Christ's salvation as an absolutely free gift, whereas the latter is disposed to receive only a part of it, and that upon the ground of his own repentance and faith.

Hence also we may discern what we are to understand by the sorrow of the world. 'Godly sorrow', says the apostle Paul, 'worketh repentance to salvation not to be repented of; but the sorrow of the world worketh death' (2 *Cor.* 2:10). How great is the difference between the sorrow of the evangelical and that of the legal penitent! The one is a sorrow according to God: the other is the sorrow of the world. The former works repentance unto life: the latter works death. Now what is the sorrow of the world? It is that legal sorrow, accompanied by horror of conscience, which the men of the world sometimes have and which arises from a dread of God as a vindictive Judge, ready to take vengeance on them for their crimes, and that, without any apprehension of his mercy in Christ. This is nothing but the beginning of eternal death, of inconceivable and endless anguish in the fire that shall never be quenched. It is also that impatient vexation which worldlings often feel for the loss of worldly things or for disappointment in the gratification of worldly lusts. Now this sorrow likewise works death, temporal and eternal death. It often brings diseases on the body which terminate in death; and sometimes, as in the case of Ahithophel and Judas, it makes men lay violent hands upon themselves. It works in them a dreadful apprehension of eternal death, and, if sovereign grace prevent not, issues in it. The sorrow of the world is indeed a killing sorrow. While it is prejudicial to the precious soul, it injures the body and hastens death. Reader, the more godly sorrow for sin you attain, the more shall you be elevated above worldly sorrow. The former is the antidote to the latter. And if you would advance in the exercise of godly sorrow, trust firmly in Jesus Christ for pardoning mercy and sanctifying grace, and see that your grief on any worldly account always terminates in sorrow for sin.

From what has been said it is evident that a legal repentance is very far from being a true one. It is far from being spiritual and acceptable to the Lord; and therefore, a man may attain the highest degree of it and after all perish as Cain, Pharaoh, and Judas did. It fills, indeed, the conscience with trouble under the dread of God's infinite wrath, but it leaves the heart under the dominion and love of sin. In the exercise of legal repentance, the sinner mourns for sin only as it has wounded his own soul; which shows that his remorse flows merely from a natural spring, and rises only to a natural height. But in the exercise of evangelical repentance, the believer mourns for sin as it has wounded his dear Redeemer, as it has pierced that heart which loves him, and spilled that blood which redeems him. This is an evidence that his sorrow for sin has its spring above nature, and that it rises to a supernatural height. Legal repentance springs only from nature and in its exercise rises no higher than depraved nature. True repentance, on the contrary, proceeds from the grace of Christ, and in its exercise aims chiefly at the glory of Christ, and of God in him. Ah, how blind must that sinner be who mistakes a legal for an evangelical repentance, and who flatters himself that he is in a state of salvation merely because he exercises a natural and legal repentance!

In conclusion: It is evident from what has been stated, that great care is requisite for distinguishing well between true repentance and that which is legal and counterfeit. This is of immense importance, seeing that many who live and die impenitent sometimes appeared penitent, both in their own view and in that of others. True repentance, as already observed, is a change of mind, inclination, and affection, with respect to sin, to God and his law, to Christ and his gospel, and to the sinner himself. From this change proceed godly sorrow for sin, detestation of it, and turning from it to the love, service, and enjoyment of God in Christ. Without this supernatural change and its immediate effects, no other appearances, whether of legal terror, or of supposed humiliation, whilst all sin is not hated and forsaken, nor universal holiness loved and practised, are sincere or acceptable to God. A man may mourn bitterly for sin and yet not mourn spiritually for it. True mourning for sin is more for the evil that is in it than for the evil which comes by it; more because it dishonours God and wounds Christ and grieves the Holy Spirit, and deprives the soul of the image of God, than because it exposes the soul to eternal punishment. A man may also hate sin and yet be far from exercising true repentance. He may abhor iniquity more in others than in himself, whereas the true penitent hates sin more in himself than in any other.

A man may abhor sin more for the shame which attends it than for the malignity and odiousness which are in it; and he may hate one sin because it is contrary to another which he loves dearly. The sincere penitent, on the contrary, hates all sin as sin, and abhors it chiefly for the evil that is in it. A man may even forsake most of his transgressions without exercising true repentance. If he forsake open, and yet retain secret sins, or if he leave sin and yet continue to love it, or if he let one sin go in order to hold another the faster, or if he forsake sin, but not as sin, he is not a true penitent. He who forsakes any sin as sin, or because it is sin, relinquishes all sin. The sincere penitent forsakes all iniquity from right principles, by right motives, in a right manner, and to a right end. Let every man take heed, then, that he do not impose upon himself by mistaking a false for a true repentance. And if he begin to suspect that his repentance is legal and counterfeit, let him without delay trust cordially in Jesus Christ for grace to exercise evangelical repentance.

5: THE FRUITS AND EVIDENCES OF TRUE REPENTANCE

When John the Baptist saw many of the Pharisees and Sadducees coming to his Baptism, he said to them, 'Bring forth fruits meet for repentance' (*Matt.* 3:8). What he styles fruits the apostle Paul calls works, meet for repentance (*Acts* 26:20). The fruits of true repentance, then, are in general the good works which every evangelical penitent endeavours, through grace, diligently to perform; the spiritual and acceptable works, or 'fruits of righteousness, which are by Jesus Christ, to the glory and praise of God' (*Phil.* 1:11). They are styled fruits, and fruits of repentance, for they spring from the incorruptible seed of evangelical repentance in the heart, implanted there at regeneration. Such works, are 'fruits meet for repentance'. They are suitable to it, and they evince the genuineness of it. As a tree is known by its fruit, so repentance is known by good works. These are effects of it, and therefore are proofs or evidences to men of the sincerity of it. The root of true repentance is in the heart. But in vain does a man pretend to have it there, if the fruit of spiritual exercises and of holy performances does not appear in the life. Even though Cain's terror, Pharaoh's fair promises, Ahab's humiliation, Herod's reverencing the prophet, hearing him gladly, and doing many things, Judas' confession, the stony-ground hearers' joy, the tongues of men and of angels, the gifts of miracles and of prophecy, and the knowledge of all mysteries, were all concentrated in one man, they would not prove him to be a true penitent. Nothing can evince this except the genuine fruits of evangelical repentance. The chief of these I shall now consider briefly, under the following particulars:

1. *Carefulness or vigilance is one of the fruits of it.*

'Behold', said the apostle to the Corinthians, 'this self-same thing, that ye sorrowed after a godly sort, what carefulness it wrought in you' (*2 Cor.* 7:11). The exercise of their godly sorrow produced in them a holy thoughtfulness and care to comply with the apostle's injunctions with respect to the incestuous person, and to approve themselves to God by rectifying what was amiss. It rendered them careful to remove him from visible communion with them, of which they had been negligent before, and to sin after this fashion no more; and solicitous also to perform good works in general, as well as not to displease the Lord. Carefulness about the one thing needful, that good part which shall not be taken away, is both a fruit and an evidence of evangelical repentance. The true penitent is careful to keep himself from his iniquity, and to 'walk worthy of the Lord to all pleasing' (*Col.* 1:10).

2. *Another of the fruits of true repentance is the penitent's clearing of himself.*

Our apostle, in the passage already cited, adds, 'Yea, what clearing of yourselves!', as if he had said, 'Your godly sorrow influenced you to take such measures with respect to the incestuous person, as might furnish a plea against any accusation of connivance with him in his guilt.' The believers in Corinth cleared themselves, not by denying the fact, or defending it, but by confessing their culpable neglect, declaring that they did not approve of the sin, but abhorred it, and that they complied willingly with the apostle's directions. Every sincere penitent, by relying only on the surety-righteousness of Jesus Christ for his title to the justification of life, clears himself in the sight of God from all the guilt of his own sins (*Isa.* 45:24); and by refusing to countenance sinful principles and practices around him, he clears himself from being partaker of other men's sins. He studies also to clear his character from slanderous imputations of evil, or even of doubtful conduct.

3. *Holy indignation against sin is a fruit and evidence of evangelical repentance.*

The apostle in the fore-cited passage adds, 'Yea, what indignation!' The godly sorrow of the saints in Corinth raised in their souls a holy indignation, a lively resentment, against their own iniquities, and against the sin of that delinquent who had publicly dishonoured the name of Christ, and had both defiled and troubled the church.

It excited indignation in them, not against the person of the offender, but against his heinous sin, and not his only, but their own also, in not excluding him from their communion sooner. The heart of every true penitent is filled with indignation against his iniquities, as striking immediately against the honour of his God and Saviour (*Psa.* 51:4 with *Psa.* 119:104). Godly sorrow for sin makes the heart of the penitent rise and swell with indignation at sin, and at himself as a sinner. The more he is enabled to trust that God for Christ's sake forgives him, the less able is he to forgive himself. He is angry and sins not, when he is angry at nothing but sin, and angry with himself only because he has sinned.

4. *Another consequence and evidence of true repentance, according to the apostle, is fear, a filial and reverential fear of God, which causes the soul to stand in awe of God, and holds it back from that which would offend and dishonour him* (Gen. 39:9).

The penitential sorrow of the Corinthians wrought in them, not a slavish fear of hell, but a filial fear of God; a fear of sinning against him, and of grieving his Spirit and his ministers; a fear lest, as the apostle had suggested, the contagion should spread in the church; a jealous and cautious fear, lest any accursed thing should still be found with them, or lest, by the force of temptation, they should fall into a similar or any other abomination, to provoke the Lord to anger. The true penitent fears lest he offend; and that he may not offend, he exercises a holy and filial fear of God, and a humble and jealous fear of himself. There arises in his heart a reverential fear from an awful apprehension of the infinite majesty and holiness of the Lord; and also a fear which makes him vigilant, disposing him to watch and war against sin, that it may not, in time to come, surprise and prevail against him.

5. *Vehement or ardent desire, is one of the fruits of evangelical repentance.*

When the believers in Corinth sorrowed to repentance, it produced in them, as the apostle says, 'vehement desire'. It excited in them fervent desire after a thorough reformation, by putting away from among them that wicked person and every evil thing (*1 Cor.* 5:13), and by doing what would be well pleasing to God through Jesus Christ. It raised in them an ardent desire to give the apostle full satisfaction, and to honour God for the future by a holy and exemplary conduct. True repentance, in whomsoever it is, produces not merely desire, but vehement desire to depart from all iniquity, to exercise all spiritual graces, and to perform all commanded duties, as well as to advance daily in conformity to Jesus Christ, and in communion with him (*Psa.* 27:4). A false penitent may pray in secret, but the true penitent must. His vehement desire cannot be shut up within him. It must have a vent; and it cannot vent itself otherwise than by the prayer of faith. Happy are they who are thus necessitated to wrestle daily with the Lord in secret!

6. The apostle informs us, in the passage already cited, that godly sorrow produces zeal.

Under the influences of the Holy Spirit, it inflamed the hearts of the saints in Corinth with ardent zeal for the manifested glory of God in Christ; for restoring the discipline, peace, and order of the church; for the doctrines of grace, and the ordinances of the gospel; and for defending the character of the apostle against the slanders of the false teachers. Wherever evangelical repentance exists it produces that sacred zeal which is according to knowledge, an enlightened zeal for the glory of God and the interest of Christ in the world (*Psa.* 137:5-6). This holy zeal is an affection compounded of love and anger. It is an enlightened and prudent eagerness of spirit to honour God, to promote true holiness, and to oppose error and wickedness (*Num.* 25:13). The zealous penitent, from a tender regard to the honour of God his Saviour, burns with holy anger against all corruptions of his truth and transgressions of his law, exerts himself to advance his glory among men, and to transmit to the latest posterity, entire and uncorrupted, the doctrines and ordinances of his glorious gospel. He may be compared to the burning bush. It was sharp indeed and prickly, but was so in the midst of light and heat. He sees transgressors and is grieved. He loves the Lord, and therefore hates evil. It is not the persons of transgressors that he abhors, but their sins. His zeal begins at home. He diligently strives against, and suppresses, those sins in himself against which he declares in others around him. He remembers that, as the snuffers in the temple were of pure gold, so they who would be zealous for pure religion in others, ought to be pure themselves. Having turned to the love and practice of a new obedience, he is zealous for good works, and careful to maintain them.

7. *Another of the fruits of true repentance is revenge on sin.*

Our apostle in the fore-cited passage says that the godly sorrow of the Corinthians wrought revenge in them. It disposed them to take a sort of holy vengeance upon themselves, like men who know not how to forgive themselves, when they reflected on the malignity and heinousness of their own sins; and it made them determined to inflict deserved punishment on the scandalous delinquent by casting him out of the church. It produced in them, not revenge on persons in a private way, for such vengeance belongs to God, but a readiness to revenge, by the infliction of church-censures, all disobedience, particularly that of the unhappy offender among them, which was shown in the punishment inflicted on him by many. Godly sorrow and self-loathing reveal themselves by holy revenge; such revenge, especially on the body of sin in the heart, as aims at the complete destruction of it. How great was that revenge on the body of sin, which the apostle Paul felt, when he exclaimed, 'O wretched man that I am! who shall deliver me from the body of this death?' (*Rom.* 7:24). He who formerly delighted in sin is now divided against himself. He now acts the part of an accuser, advocate, and judge, against himself: yea, he, as it were, inflicts punishment on himself for the exceeding sinfulness of his heart and life. Accordingly, the humble penitent is represented as smiting on his thigh (*Jer.* 31:19), as if he thereby declared that he would willingly take vengeance on the legs that carried him forward in the ways of sin; and that he would be filled with holy resentment against himself for the innumerable injuries which, by his unaccountable crimes, he did to the honour of his God and Saviour. When he repents of his wickedness, he says, 'What have I done?' (*Jer.* 8:6). What an ungrateful, what a vile, what a loathsome, what a wretched sinner, have I been!

8. *The penitent's making ample restitution of what he borrowed or fraudulently took from others is a fruit and evidence of true repentance.*

According to the ceremonial law, the trespass-offering was to be accompanied by restitution to the party who had been injured (*Lev.* 6:1-5). Zacchaeus, accordingly, proved himself a true penitent by making ample restitution. Every sincere penitent will likewise, with self-loathing, make haste to rid himself of dishonest gain. He will shake his hands from holding of bribes (*Isa.* 33:15). He will obey scrupulously the charge of Solomon: 'Withhold not good from them to whom it is due, when it is in the power of thine hand to do it' (*Prov.* 3:27). With diligence he will make search for every remainder of that accursed thing. With interest, he will restore it to the injured party if he can; if not, to their relations; and failing them, to the poor. And if he be not able, it will occasion much uneasiness and distress of mind to him. He who has injured his neighbour, and refuses, though he has ability, to make restitution, is an unrighteous man; and 'the unrighteous shall not inherit the kingdom of God' (*1 Cor.* 6:9). All appearances of repentance without this are hypocritical. Whatever profession of repentance such a man makes, his religion is vain. He refuses to do to others as he would that they should do to him. To pretend to have turned from iniquity with bitter remorse, and yet to feed sweetly on the fruits of it, is vain. This is so obvious that even Judas in his repentance, counterfeit as it was, was impelled to restore the reward of iniquity.

An ancient philosopher at Athens, having, at a shop there, obtained a pair of shoes with promise to pay for them at a later date, and having afterwards heard that the tradesman was dead, at first was glad to think that the debt was now paid. But recollecting himself, he brought the money and threw it into the shop, saying, 'Take it; thou art alive to me, while dead to all the world besides.' What, then, are we to think of many professed Christians who see their creditors struggling with those difficulties into which their extravagance has plunged them, while they themselves are in easy, perhaps in affluent circumstances, and so are well able, if they choose to retrench superfluous expenses, to make them restitution in whole or in part, but will not, because not compelled by law? Such persons show themselves to be destitute of true repentance, for they prefer wealth, indulgence, and the pride of life, to rendering 'to all their dues', to owing no man any thing, but to love him (*Rom.* 13:7-8). They who can restore that which they owe their neighbour, but will not, surely do not turn from that sin, for they deliberately continue to enjoy the fruit of it.

9. *Another of the fruits and evidences of evangelical repentance is the reparation of injuries in cases in which proper restitution cannot be made; such as injuries done to persons in their reputation, in their influence and usefulness, in their families or connections, in their peace of mind, in their contentment, and in many other instances.*

Hence is this exhortation: 'Confess your faults one to another' (*James* 5:16). The evangelical penitent, though he cannot undo what he has done yet will study to counteract the evil arising from the injury, by stooping even to the humblest submissions, and the most ingenuous confessions, how contrary soever to the pride and self-love remaining in his heart. If he was formerly guilty of such scandalous offences as impaired the honour of God before the world, exposed religion to the scorn of profane men, and grieved or stumbled the hearts of the godly he will endeavour diligently to counteract the tendency of his former evil conduct. Or if he formerly propagated errors respecting either doctrine or duty, he will now retract them, and exert himself to undo that part of his conduct. And as far as his arguments, his persuasions, his influence and example can reach, he will diligently endeavour to stop the further progress of the mischief. In these and various other instances, true repentance, under the almighty agency of the Holy Spirit, disposes a man to employ every proper means of counteracting the tendency of his former bad conduct. Indeed, to repent sincerely of such injuries, and yet wilfully to refuse the conduct by which the honour of God and the credit of religion may in some measure be restored, is impossible. A man may as well pretend to repent of his having wounded a person, whilst he sees him bleeding to death, and yet refuses, though he has it in his power, to bind up his wounds. Multitudes, alas, flatter themselves that they have sincerely repented of their sins, who yet will on no account condescend to make the smallest reparation for the injuries they have done. This indeed shows that their penitence is no better than that of Ahab, who humbled himself, but neither restored Naboth's vineyard, nor turned from any of his other abominations.

10. *Once more, diligence in the spiritual performance of all our duties is one of the fruits of true repentance.*

To be diligent is to be bent on activity, constant in application, and persevering in endeavour. The evangelical penitent, under the sanctifying influences of the Holy Spirit, and in proportion to the degree of his repentance, performs all his duties with speed, activity, and perseverance. When he remembers, with sorrow and self-abasement, how diligent he was in the service of sin and Satan, how he did evil with both hands earnestly (*Mic.* 7:3), he is powerfully urged to serve now with holy diligence his God and Saviour. And especially when he considers how diligent his adorable Redeemer was in obeying the law as a covenant, for his justification, he is irresistibly constrained to give all diligence in yielding obedience to it as a rule, for his glory. He is commanded, not only to keep the commandments of this holy law as the rule of his duty, but to keep them diligently. 'Ye shall diligently keep the commandments of the LORD your God' (*Deut.* 6:17). And again, 'Thou hast commanded us to keep thy precepts diligently' (*Psa.* 119:4). The true penitent, accordingly, is diligent in all his duties, not only in all the various duties of his civil calling, but in the exercises of devotion in all their variety. In the latter he is even more diligent than in the former. As the shekel of the sanctuary was the double of the common shekel, so, in the affairs of eternity, he doubles the diligence that he uses in the business of time. Like Solomon, he first builds the house of God, and then his own house. He looks upon the salvation of his soul, in subservience to the manifested glory of God, as the most interesting employment of life. And therefore he not only gives diligence, but all diligence, in adding 'to his faith, virtue; and to virtue, knowledge; and to knowledge, temperance; and to temperance, patience; and to patience, godliness; and to godliness, brotherly kindness; and to brotherly kindness, charity' (2 *Pet.* 1:5-7).

So much for the principal fruits and evidences of true repentance.

✜

Reader, have you in any degree brought forth these fruits of evangelical repentance? If you have, they are so many evidences of your having the grace of true repentance. They are signs of your having that repentance to salvation which is not to be repented of. They are so many proofs that you have in regeneration received the principle of this repentance, and that in progressive sanctification you have attained the habit and exercise of it. They are, therefore, great encouragements to you to continue and advance in the daily exercise of it, and by faith to receive more and more of it out of the fullness of Christ. But, although they serve to encourage you to these, yet they form no part of your warrant to trust in Christ for that great salvation, of which evangelical repentance is an essential part. Your warrant to renew the exercise of trusting in Jesus Christ for his whole salvation, lies in his word of grace, and not in either your heart or your life (*John* 3:27). And therefore, if you make your evidences of grace your warrant or ground of right, either in whole or in part, to renew the acting of faith in Christ, you will provoke him to hide his face, and to cover them with a cloud in his anger. They are fruits, not only of repentance, but of faith; but if you presume to make them grounds of faith, your faith and repentance will quickly decline. See that your exercise of faith, then, be always grounded on faithfulness in the Word, and never on feelings in the heart. True repentance is offered and promised to you in the blessed gospel. Trust in the Lord Jesus for it, on the warrant of the unlimited offer and promise. Trust also and plead this precious and absolute promise: 'All the ends of the world shall remember and turn unto the LORD' (*Psa.* 22:27). Place at all times the confidence of your heart in Jesus Christ, and rely with firm trust on his faithfulness in that promise, for the performance of it to you; and according to your faith it will be unto you. He will make you advance daily in the habit and exercise of repentance unto life.

Let every reader endeavour diligently to repent, and to bring forth fruits worthy of true repentance. Advance daily in those holy tempers, and in the performance of those good works, which are the fruits of evangelical repentance. Since the genuine fruits of evangelical repentance are at the same time works of faith and labours of love, it will be necessary that you exercise faith and love in order to produce them. The exercise of unfeigned faith and love is pre-requisite to true repentance, and to all the genuine fruits of it. As these fruits are fruits also 'of righteousness, which are by Jesus Christ, to the glory and praise of God' (*Phil.* 1:11), it will be no less necessary for their production, that you be united to Christ, that you have his righteousness imputed to you, and his Spirit as a Spirit of holiness put within you. And as they are fruit unto God, you must be dead to the law as a covenant of works, as well as united to Christ, in order to produce even the smallest measure of them. Paul addressed the believers in Rome thus: 'Ye also are become dead to the law by the body of Christ; that ye should be married to another, even to him who is raised from the dead, that we should bring forth fruit unto God' (*Rom.* 7:4). To be united in a conjugal relation to Christ, the head and husband of his church, and to be delivered in justification from the law as a covenant of works, are necessary to your bringing forth fruit unto God, or your serving him in newness of spirit. O consider, then, that it will be impossible for you, either to exercise true repentance, or to bring forth any of its fruits, unless, in order to do so, you are a believer in Jesus Christ, united to him by faith, justified by his righteousness imputed to you, and dead to the law as a covenant. All these are necessary to the least exercise of evangelical repentance and to the production of any of its fruits. Come to Christ, then, for grace and strength to exercise true repentance. Believe on him in order to repent sincerely. The more you cordially trust in him for the grace of repentance, the more you will repent of all your sins; and the more you sincerely repent of them, the more of the fruits of repentance will you produce. Your exercise of repentance will be according to your acting of faith.

6: The Priority of the Acting of Saving Faith to the Exercise of True Repentance

In the moment of regeneration the Holy Spirit implants all spiritual and saving graces in the heart of the elect sinner, and among others, faith and repentance. He implants at the same instant the root or principle of saving faith and of true repentance. He gives these two graces together and at once in respect of time; and therefore, though in our conception of them, they are to be distinguished, yet they are never to be separated from each other. The principle of faith in the regenerate soul, that is, the capacity of acting faith, is not in point of time before that of repentance, nor is the principle of repentance before that of faith. Every true believer in principle is at the same time a true penitent, and every true penitent in respect of principle is a genuine believer. An impenitent believer, and a penitent unbeliever, are characters which have no existence but in the vain imaginations of some men. But, though the principle of saving faith does not in respect of time precede that of true repentance, yet in order of nature, the acting of that faith precedes the exercise of this repentance (*Zech.* 12:10). The regenerate sinner is enabled cordially to apprehend or trust in the pardoning mercy of God in Christ, in order to exercise true repentance (*Psa.* 13:5). For he cannot begin to exercise that repentance which is spiritual and acceptable to God until he first begin to trust cordially in Jesus Christ for mercy and grace. The exercise of true repentance, as already observed, flows from that of justifying and saving faith. A legal and counterfeit repentance, indeed, often goes before the first acting of true faith; but the exercise of evangelical or true repentance never goes before, but always springs from it and follows it. The exercise of true faith is the instrument or means of attaining, through grace, the habit and exercise of evangelical repentance. The first acting of saving faith in conversion is the means of attaining the first exercise of that repentance; and the renewed actings of that precious faith are the means of being enabled to renew the exercise of it.

Seeing the priority of the acting of unfeigned faith to the exercise of true repentance is of immense importance to the holiness and comfort of believers, in subordination to the glory of God, I shall endeavour to evince the reality of it by the following arguments:

1. *Faith is the principal grace, and the acting of it is the first breathing, the first vital motion of the regenerate soul.*

No sooner is the dead sinner quickened than he begins to act spiritually, and his first activity is that of believing.

His true belief of the law with application to himself issues in true conviction of his sinfulness of heart and life, and also in something resembling legal repentance; and his saving faith of the gospel with application to himself issues in union and communion with Christ, and so in evangelical repentance. Without faith it is impossible to please God (*Heb.* 11:6); and therefore it is impossible, without the previous exercise of it, so to repent as to please him (*Jer.* 31:19-20). 'Without me', says the Lord Jesus, 'ye can do nothing' (*John* 15:5). If, separate from Christ or without vital union with him by faith, a man can do nothing that is spiritually good, we may be sure that without it he cannot exercise spiritual repentance. Such repentance is usually styled evangelical, because the exercise of it is attained by faith in Jesus Christ as exhibited to sinners in the gospel. Though the law, in the hand of the Spirit, serves in a good degree to reveal the inexpressible malignity, odiousness, and demerit of sin, yet the glorious gospel affords brighter and more affecting discoveries of these. It is in this glass that the true penitent attains the most humbling and heart-melting views of the exceeding sinfulness of sin; such views of it as, under the influences of the Holy Spirit, will bring godly sorrow to the heart and the tears of evangelical repentance to the eyes. It is the eye of faith, contemplating sin in the cross of the adorable Redeemer that affects the heart with bitter repentance and with true abhorrence of all iniquity.

2. *Saving faith is the leading grace, especially to the exercise of true repentance.*

The acting of the former is in order to the exercise of the latter. Accordingly we read in the Scripture, That 'a great number believed, and turned unto the Lord' (*Acts* 11:21), and that the house of David, and the inhabitants of Jerusalem shall look upon him whom they have pierced, and shall mourn for him (*Zech.* 12:10). The tears of godly sorrow drop as it were from the eye of faith. It is the exercise of faith in the crucified Redeemer that melts the hard heart into penitential mourning, and that produces the tears which run down in repentance. The eye of faith fixes on God in Christ as a God of love, mercy, and grace; and then by repentance the heart turns to him, and to the love and practice of true holiness (*Jer.* 3:22). A godly minister, accordingly, gives us this admonition:

> When you go to mourn for sin, begin aloft with Christ; and do not think to begin below with sin, and so to come up to Christ; but being aloft with Christ, and fall down upon your sin.

True repentance is our turning to God. But if the exercise of this repentance were before that of faith, sinners might return to God without coming by Christ as the only way to him, contrary to this declaration of Christ respecting himself: 'I am the way . . . no man cometh unto the Father but by me' (*John* 14:6). Evangelical repentance cannot otherwise be attained than by faith receiving it from the Lord Jesus, who is exalted to give it (*Acts* 5:31).

3. *The exercise of true repentance flows immediately from unfeigned love to Christ, and to God in him; but such love to him springs from the exercise of true faith on him.*

The exercise of evangelical repentance, I say, flows immediately from genuine love to Jesus Christ, and to God in him. The believing sinner exercises godly sorrow for his sins, because he pierced Christ, his dear Redeemer by them. But this he could not do unless he loved Christ with a supreme and tender love. It is his ardent love of the Redeemer that, under the infinite agency of the Holy Spirit, disposes and impels him to mourn and be in bitterness for having pierced and put him to grief. Also he forsakes with deep abhorrence all his iniquities, because they are infinitely hateful to God, and because he has thereby insulted and reproached his glorious Majesty. But he could not on these accounts hate sin, if he did not love Christ and God in Christ supremely, and if he did not love sincerely the holiness of his nature and his law. Moreover, he turns to God, and to a diligent endeavour after new obedience to him. This, however, arises from superlative esteem of him, and from ardent affection to him. The exercise of true repentance, then, springs immediately from sincere love to Christ and to God in him, as an infinitely holy and gracious God.

This love flows from the exercise of unfeigned faith. It is 'faith that worketh by love' (*Gal.* 5:6). By faith the believer spiritually apprehends the love or good will of God to him. 'We have known and believed', says the apostle John, 'the love that God hath to us: God is love' (*1 John* 4:16). Calvin's remark on this passage appears to be just. 'We have known and believed', or, that is, says he,

> We have known by believing. In a preceding verse, the apostle represented faith as our believing that Jesus is the Son of God; but here he says, By faith we know the love of God toward us.

When a man cordially believes the love of God to him, he in the same degree loves God, because God first loved him (*1 John* 4:19). He believes or trusts that God loves him with a love of good will, and so, he is powerfully and sweetly constrained to love him in return. It is not the secret love of God in election, nor the secret operation of it in regeneration, that is more directly intended by the phrase, 'he first loved us'; but the public manifestation of his love in the gift of Christ as exhibited in the gospel; even that discovery of his love which is the object of the direct exercise of faith. This view of the apostle's assertion is confirmed by the fact that he uses this most sublime expression, 'GOD IS LOVE' (*1 John* 4:16). Here he intimates that God, as the object of faith, is love; and also that a convinced sinner cannot sincerely love him, till he first believes that, in Jesus Christ his dear Son, HE IS LOVE even to him. The special love of God to the believer may, indeed, be concluded from his unfeigned love to God.

But it does not follow that there is no apprehension at all of the loveliness and love of God to him, at his first exercise of love to God. The love of God in Christ, apprehended by the direct acting of faith, may well begin and promote that exercise. The believer's love to God, which is excited by the faith of God's love to him, is no more a mercenary, or a sinful self-love, than that of the Psalmist, when he loved Jehovah as his strength, his rock, his fortress and deliverer, his God, the horn of his salvation, and his high tower (*Psa.* 18:1-2). Nor is it any more a self-love than that of Paul and the believers at Corinth, when the love of Christ, manifested in his dying for them, constrained them to live not to themselves but to him. The Psalmist, by saying to the Lord, 'Whom have I in heaven but thee? and there is none upon earth that I desire besides thee' expresses his exercise of supreme love to him. But he attained this exercise of love by the acting of his faith, expressed thus in the immediately preceding verse: 'Thou shalt guide me with thy counsel, and afterward receive me to glory' (*Psa.* 73:24-25). It is evident, then, that the exercise of true repentance proceeds from supreme love to God, and that this love springs from the exercise of unfeigned faith. The acting of this faith therefore precedes the exercise of that repentance.

4. *The exercise of genuine repentance supposes true conviction of sin and misery, and this proceeds from a true faith of the law.*

Legal repentance, which is exercised by many unregenerate persons, springs from legal conviction and legal terror. But the exercise of evangelical repentance arises from that true and thorough conviction which is a consequence of that true faith of the law, implanted by the Holy Spirit at regeneration. Arising from such conviction of sin as follows upon the faith of the law, it may well be said to spring from this faith, as well as from the saving faith of the gospel. The subject of true repentance is a convinced sinner. 'He sheweth them their work, and their transgressions that they have exceeded. He openeth also their ear to discipline, and commandeth that they return from iniquity' (*Job* 36:9-10 with *Acts* 2:37-38). As soon as a sinner is regenerated, and has true faith implanted in his heart, he believes the doctrine of the law, with particular application to himself. Hence arises true conviction of sin, and this is followed by the saving faith of the gospel. The exercise of true repentance, then, in the order of nature, springs both from the true faith of the law and from the saving faith of the gospel. If it follow that faith of the gospel, it must of course follow that faith of the law from which true conviction proceeds. This faith and this conviction, therefore, are previously necessary to that exercise.

5. *Evangelical repentance is included in sanctification, and the means or instrument of sanctification, is justifying and saving faith.*

As the exercise of saving faith is, according to the covenant of grace, previously necessary to sanctification, so is it to the exercise of that repentance which is comprised in sanctification. That evangelical repentance is included in sanctification is evident. No man can repent unless he hate sin and love holiness. None can hate sin and turn from it, except he be sanctified: and none can be sanctified unless he have that saving faith, by the acting of which a man is vitally united to Christ, the head of sanctifying influences. In actual sanctification, the believer dies more and more to sin, and lives to righteousness. Now, what is it to die to sin, but to exercise godly sorrow for it, and holy abhorrence of it? And what is it to live to righteousness, but to turn to God from the love and practice of all iniquity, and to the love and practice of universal holiness? The habit of evangelical repentance is evidently contained in habitual sanctification, and the exercise of it is included in actual sanctification. The habit and the exercise of true repentance, then, have their place in habitual and actual sanctification. The principle of true repentance, indeed, as previously observed, is infused at regeneration; but the habit and exercise of it are not introduced but in sanctification. Now saving faith is the means or instrument of sanctification. Accordingly we read in Scripture that they who are sanctified, 'are sanctified by faith' (*Acts* 26:18). The first acting of that faith must be before the first exercise of this repentance, as the means are before, and in order to the end.

6. *If the exercise of true repentance be previously requisite, or preparatory, to the first acting of saving faith, the convinced sinner must be satisfied that his repentance is true, before he begin to believe in Jesus Christ for salvation.*

Were it true that Jesus and his great salvation are, in

the gospel, offered to none but the true penitent, and that none else is warranted to receive the offer it would follow that no sinner could warrantably embrace the offer till he were previously satisfied that his repentance was not counterfeit, but true; or, that he could not without sin attempt to come to Christ, or to trust in him for salvation, until it was certified to his conscience that his repentance had all the discriminating characters of a true repentance. And seeing the exercise of genuine repentance springs from unfeigned love to God, he must be satisfied too, that he loves God sincerely, not only while he apprehends God to be his infinite enemy, but while he is indeed his enemy. The apostle Paul says that 'Whatsoever is not of faith is sin' (*Rom.* 14:23); that is, 'whatsoever is done in doubt of conscience, whether God has commanded it or not, is sin.' And it is plain from the context, that by faith here, the apostle means the faith of God's command. If, then, the exercise of true repentance be a qualification previously necessary to the first acting of saving faith, and if the convinced sinner cannot be satisfied that his repentance is of the true kind, or that God commands him in particular to believe in Christ how can he, so long as he doubts whether the command affording him a warrant for believing be addressed to him, attempt to believe in the Saviour? He may be sure that his attempting an act of faith, whilst he doubts his warrant for it, is his sin.

No wonder that the convinced and affrighted sinner doubts if he be a true penitent, and that he is ready to conclude he is not! But until he be satisfied that his repentance is of the true kind, he must not, according to that doctrine, presume to trust in the Saviour for salvation. If the Lord invites none to share in the provisions of his house but the true penitent, then he that doubteth is condemned if he eat. As the sinner cannot see any thing that is spiritually good in himself before, but only in, or after, his first exercise of faith, it will be impossible for him ever to act faith on Christ warrantably; because true repentance, supposing him to have the principle of it, cannot be seen by him before his first acting of faith. Consequently no sinner in the world could ever begin lawfully to trust in the Saviour for salvation. For none must presume to trust in Christ until he see that he is a true penitent; and this cannot be discerned till he have already begun to believe or trust in him.

But is it true that the offers of the gospel, and the commandment to believe in Jesus Christ, are addressed to none but true penitents? Far from it. Christ with his righteousness and salvation is in the gospel offered to sinners of mankind in common—to sinners as such; and sinners as such are invited and commanded to believe on his name (*John* 3:23); 'Whosoever will, let him take the water of life freely' (Rev. 22:17). 'Whosoever believeth in him shall not perish, but have everlasting life' (*John* 3:16).

The error which has now been adverted to, is most injurious to such as are seeking Jesus, and fighting against unbelief; for it tends greatly to discourage, and even to obstruct, all their attempts to trust in him for salvation from sin and wrath. Although they apprehend the wrath of God denounced against them for their innumerable transgressions, and hear of a free salvation offered in the gospel, yet it still appears to be forbidden fruit to them, because they are far from being certain that they have exercised true repentance. For they consider the exercise of true repentance to be a pre-requisite qualification for the acting of unfeigned faith. Hence the offers of a compassionate Saviour, and the promises of a great salvation, do but torment them the more; while they falsely persuade themselves that none but the true penitent has a right to apply and trust them. As they cannot be satisfied before the first acting of faith that their exercise of repentance is genuine, and as they cannot attain deliverance from their perplexing fears, nor victory over the least of their spiritual enemies, but by the exercise of faith in the almighty Redeemer, their souls are ensnared, and obstructed in faith, in holiness, and in comfort. So long as they adhere to this false persuasion, it will effectually deter them from coming as sinners to Christ, and from trusting in him, so as to be filled 'with all joy and peace in believing' (*Rom.* 15:13).

Are you entangled in this perplexing snare? Do you persuade yourself that the exercise of true repentance, and a consciousness of this exercise, are previously necessary to the acting of unfeigned faith? Do you postpone the act of trusting in the Lord Jesus for all his salvation, till you first sit down and mourn a while for your sins, or till your heart be so humbled that you may be welcome to him, and so have from your own resources a warrant for trusting in him? Do you object against coming to Christ, because you are not certain that your conviction of sin and your repentance are of the right sort? Do you apply yourself to the exercise of repentance in order to be qualified for believing in Christ, or do you apply your conscience to the commands and curses of the broken law, in order so to repent as to be entitled to trust in him? Know, I intreat you, that this preposterous and self-righteous course will but sink you the deeper in unbelief, impenitence, and enmity to God. The longer you try in this manner to seek for evangelical repentance in your heart or life, the farther you will be from finding it.

But perhaps you will reply, Can any man who is not a true penitent exercise a saving faith in Christ? I answer, No, he cannot. But though no man can act a saving faith without having the principle of true repentance, or a disposition to exercise it, implanted by the Holy Spirit in his heart, yet multitudes have believed, and do believe to the saving of the soul, without having previously seen that they had that principle, and without any previous exercise of it. To have it is necessary to the acting of true faith; but to know that you have it, is not necessary. To have the capacity or disposition to exercise true repentance is indispensably requisite; but the actual exercise of it, and your consciousness of that exercise, are not previously necessary. Study then, in dependence on the grace of the promise, and study resolutely, to believe in order to repent; to come as an unworthy and undone sinner, and, believing cordially that the offers of the gospel are directed to you in particular, to trust firmly in Jesus Christ for all his salvation, and for true repentance as an essential part of it. So shall you be enabled to exercise that evangelical repentance which will not need to be repented of. Do not try to wash yourself clean in order to come to the open fountain of redeeming blood; but come to it as you are, and, by the immediate exercise of direct confidence in the Lord Jesus, wash away all your sins (*Ezek.* 36:25).

7. *The exercise of true repentance itself shows plainly that the acting of saving faith is prior to it.*

Such repentance is a sinner's turning cordially from all sin to God. But it is impossible to turn to God except through Christ. 'I am the way [said Jesus] . . . no man cometh unto the Father but by me' (*John* 14:6). It is impossible to come to Christ and walk in him, but by the acting of faith (*John* 6:35). The sinner, then, who would turn and come to God by true repentance, must needs take Christ by faith as his way to him. He must believe or trust in Christ in order to return and come to God by Christ. The exercise of faith, therefore, is, in order of nature, before that of repentance. Repentance is, indeed, in Scripture, placed sometimes before faith. But the reason seems to be that repentance is the end, and faith the means of attaining to that end. The end is first in intention, and therefore is mentioned first; but the means are first in practice. Thus in Mark 1:15 our Lord commands sinners to repent; and in order to their exercise of repentance, he enjoins them to believe the gospel as the means of attaining that important end. The apostle Paul, said to the elders of the church at Ephesus, that he had testified to them, 'repentance toward God, and faith toward our Lord Jesus Christ' (*Acts* 20:21),—repentance toward God as the end, and faith toward our Lord Jesus Christ as the means of attaining that end. Hence it is obvious that, if faith toward our Lord Jesus Christ be not the means of attaining repentance toward God, the fundamental truth, that no man comes to the Father but by Christ, is over-turned (*John* 14:6). Were the exercise of true repentance before the acting of genuine faith, sinners might return to God without coming by Christ, the only way to him. But according to the Scriptures, the exercise of evangelical re-pentance is not otherwise to be attained than by faith, by which we look upon him whom we have pierced (*Zech.* 12:10), and by which we receive out of his fullness grace to repent. It is the cordial exercise of particular trust in the Redeemer, that, through grace, powerfully withdraws the affections from all iniquity and sweetly attaches them to the holy and blessed God. After Ezra had prayed and confessed, the people indeed wept; but they did not attempt to put away their strange wives, until Shechaniah had cried, 'We have trespassed against our God: . . . yet now there is hope in Israel concerning this thing' (*Ezra* 10:2). They who will turn must not only be prisoners of fear, but 'prisoners of hope'.

8. *Once more, the Scriptures set forth the blessed object of faith, and the precious promises of grace, as powerful motives to the exercise of true repentance.*

By this it is evident that it must be by a faith-view of that glorious object, brought near in the offers and promises, that a convinced sinner is incited and enabled, to exercise evangelical repentance. Various passages of Scripture, such as the following, set forth the exceeding riches of the grace of God, in order to excite and encourage sinners to the exercise of true repentance. 'Turn, O backsliding children, saith the LORD, for I am married unto you' (*Jer.* 3:14). 'Return, ye backsliding children, and I will heal your backslidings. Behold, we come unto thee; for thou art the LORD our God' (*Jer.* 3:22). 'Come, and let us return unto the LORD: for he hath torn, and he will heal us; he hath smitten, and he will bind us up' (*Hos.* 6:1). 'O Israel, return unto the LORD thy God; for thou hast fallen by thine iniquity' (*Hos.* 14:1). 'Therefore also now, saith the LORD, turn ye even to me with all your heart, and with fasting, and with weeping, and with mourning; and rend your heart, and not your garments, and turn unto the LORD your God: for he is gracious and merciful, slow to anger, and of great kindness' (*Joel* 1:12-13). The moral law of Sinai, which requires true repentance, is prefaced by this most gracious declaration to encourage the Israelite to obedience — 'I am the LORD thy God, *etc.*' (*Exod.* 20:2). And in the New Testament, sinners are exhorted to repentance thus: 'Repent ye, for the kingdom of heaven is at hand' (*Matt.* 3:2; 4:17). Now if the exercise of true repentance precedes that of saving faith, such passages tend to deceive us. For, by the most natural construction of them, we are induced to believe that it is by means of a previous apprehension by faith of the mercy and grace of God in Christ, that sinners are brought to the exercise of evangelical repentance. Such passages, especially when compared, show plainly that it is by a believing application of the offers and promises of the blessed gospel, and by a cordial trust in the Lord Jesus for mercy and grace, that convinced sinners are disposed to exercise true repentance.

By the arguments here advanced, it is, I trust, evident to the impartial reader that the acting of true or saving faith is, in order of nature, previous to the exercise of evangelical repentance.

Is the first act of justifying and saving faith previous, in order of nature, to the first exercise of evangelical repentance, and is the renewed acting of the former before the renewed exercise of the latter? Then the believing sinner should, in repenting of his sins, begin with the sin of unbelief. He ought, in the faith of pardoning mercy, to repent of his unbelief and distrust of the faithful Redeemer, in order to repent of all his other sins. As faith, with respect to its office in the new covenant, is the principal, the leading grace, so unbelief is the radical, the leading sin. Accordingly, when the Holy Spirit convinces an elect sinner of sin, he convinces him particularly of his unbelief (*1 John* 16:8-9). He shows him the exceeding sinfulness, hatefulness, and demerit of all his iniquities, and especially of his disbelief, and distrust of the Divine Redeemer. The exercise of evangelical repentance, therefore, has respect chiefly to this radical sin, which is the root of every other abomination. All other iniquities are but so many malignant streams issuing from unbelief as their fountain. The legal penitent, as he is never truly convinced of the strength and sinfulness of his unbelief, so he never sincerely repents of it; and because he never truly repents of that sin, he cannot repent evangelically of any other. His pretending to repent of his other transgressions is vain, so long as he does not repent of his unbelief, the corrupt fountain from which they all flow. The evangelical penitent, on the contrary, shows that his repentance is true, by repenting of all the polluted streams of his iniquities, not only in themselves but in their fountain. And if at any time, in his exercise of repentance, he overlooks his remaining unbelief, or distrust of the Saviour, he will find that his exercise of it will languish, and that hardness and impenitence of heart will prevail against him. The stronger his faith is, and the more frequently he exercises it, the more deeply he will repent of his remaining unbelief, and of all the innumerable crimes which proceed from it. Reader, see that you believe in Jesus Christ, in order to exercise true repentance, and that you repent of your unbelief, in order to repent spiritually of all your other sins. For it is in proportion as you turn from your unbelief, that root of bitterness, that you turn in an acceptable manner from any other of your iniquities.

7: THE PRIORITY OF JUSTIFICATION TO THE FIRST EXERCISE OF TRUE REPENTANCE

Before I advance arguments to prove that justification in the sight of God precedes the first exercise of true repentance, it will be necessary, in order to prevent any misconstruction of what is to be stated, that the following remarks be premised:

1. *Justification, considered as an immanent act of God, or as the eternal and unchangeable will of God to justify his elect upon the ground of a righteousness fulfilled by Christ and imputed to them, has been by judicious divines called active justification.*[1]

But justification, viewed as terminating on the persons and in the consciences of believers, has been styled passive justification. The former precedes both the principle and the first acting of true repentance. The latter takes place after regeneration, when the principle of repentance takes root in the soul but before that repentance is actually exercised. This last is the justification, which is often

---

[1] Witsius, *The Economy of the Covenants*, Book 2, Chap. 7.

mentioned in Scripture as the privilege of believers, and which is brought to pass by the instrumentality of faith (*Rom.* 3:28; *Gal.* 2:16). It is justification in this sense only that I am to consider, in its connection with the exercise of true repentance.

2. *The pardon of sin is a part of justification.*

When God is said to pardon the sins of believers, it is to be understood, first, of the act of his free grace in bringing them into an unalterable state of justification by means of faith (*Col.* 3:13); secondly, of the intimations, or the encouraging sense, which the Lord graciously affords them of their state of justification (*Psa.* 32:5); and thirdly, it is to be understood of the removal of that guilt which binds them over to those chastisements for sin which are the effects of fatherly anger. The first is included in justification, and it goes before the first exercise of evangelical repentance. The second and third do not go before, but they follow after that exercise. The first exercise of true repentance follows the forgiveness of sin in the first sense; but it goes before it in the second and third.

3. *Repentance, as has been already stated, must always be the sinner's duty.*

To deny that it is his duty to sorrow for sin, and to turn from it, would be to vindicate rebellion against the Most High. The Lord Jesus has not only said, 'Repent' (*Rev.* 3:19), but has said again and again, 'Except ye repent, ye shall perish' (*Luke* 13:3, 5).

4. *The exercise of true repentance is indispensably requisite, in all who are capable of it, as a means, without which none may expect the comfortable enjoyment of communion with God either in time or in eternity.*

It is a necessary means of spiritual consolation, and also of preparation for the perfection of eternal life.

5. *The word repentance, in the Scripture, sometimes expresses the whole of that change which takes place in the conversion of a sinner to God.*

In this sense it includes faith in Jesus Christ as well as godly sorrow for sin, and sincere endeavours to yield new obedience. It would therefore be wrong to say of repentance in this its large acceptation, that the first exercise of it is either after faith or justification. It is only of the first exercise of true repentance, taken in its strict sense, as distinct from faith and consequent upon it, that I am to speak.

6. *When I say that the first exercise of true repentance is after justification, I speak not of the order of time, but only of the order of nature; for no justified person is, or can be impenitent.*

7. *It is not of the seed or principle of evangelical repentance that I am to treat, but only of the exercise of it.*

The seed, root, or principle of true repentance, implanted at regeneration, is before justification, or the judicial pardon of sin; but the formal exercise of that repentance is, as will be shown, after it.

8. *The exercise of repentance is either legal or evangelical.*

It is either under the influence of the law as a covenant of works, and the domination of a legal spirit; or under the influence of the covenant of grace, and of an evangelical spirit. It is readily granted that legal repentance is exercised before justification; but not that which is evangelical. The first exercise of evangelical repentance does not in order of nature go before, but comes after, justification or the judicial pardon of sin.

This doctrine being understood according to these positions, I now proceed to evince the truth and importance of it by the following arguments:

1. *The first exercise of true repentance is not prior to justification in the sight of God; because there can be no acceptable performance of any good work, before this justification.*

The exercise of evangelical repentance is evidently a good work, a work which is formally as well as materially good. The description of a good work in Scripture plainly agrees to it. A good work is a work that pleases God. But the exercise of true repentance is a work which highly pleases him. When Ephraim thus repented, Jehovah said of him, 'Is Ephraim my dear son? Is he a pleasant child?' (*Jer.* 31:20). And says the Psalmist, 'The sacrifices of God are a broken spirit: a broken and a contrite heart, O God, thou wilt not despise' (*Psa.* 51:17). It may be called an evangelical work, not indeed as if it were not required in the moral law, but as it, and every other good work, is performed in reliance on the righteousness and grace of Jesus Christ. Now good works do not go before, but follow justification in the sight of God. The members of the Synod of Dort, in the 24th Article of their Confession, say:

> We are justified by faith in Christ, and that before we do good works: otherwise they could not be good works, any more than the fruit of a tree can be good before the tree itself be good.

The *Westminster Confession of Faith* says:

> Good works are fruits and evidences of a true and lively faith . . . The persons of believers being accepted through Christ, their good works are also accepted in him.

The truth of this position is evident, by observing that, according to the covenant of grace, Divine acceptance begins with the person of the believer, and then goes on to his performances. God's acceptance of his person as righteous, in the act of justification, is, in order of nature, before his acceptance of any of his works. The first exercise of true repentance is a work spiritually good and acceptable to God; and therefore, it must follow the acceptance of the person as righteous, in justification. We read that, 'The Lord had respect unto Abel and to his offering' (*Gen.* 4:4)—first, unto Abel himself, and then to his offering. The same order is abundantly evident from these words of our apostle: 'Wherefore, my brethren, ye also are become dead to the law by the body of Christ; that ye should be married to another, . . . that we should bring forth fruit unto God' (*Rom.* 7:4). Now the first, as well as the progressive, exercise of true repentance, is doubtless included in bringing forth fruit unto God. But our spiritual marriage to Christ is necessary to our bringing forth fruit unto God. In this spiritual marriage, we are dead to the law by the body of Christ; that is, we are justified, and so are delivered from the law as a covenant, by virtue of the righteousness which Christ fulfilled in our nature received by faith. Previous to this blessed change of state, the only fruit that we bring forth, is 'fruit unto death'; the only repentance that we exercise is that selfish, slavish, legal repentance, to which we are impelled by the terrors of the law and the dominion of a legal temper. The same order is also evident from the following words: 'Sin shall not have dominion over you; for ye are not under the law, but under grace' (*Rom.* 6:14). From these words we see that, while a man is under the law as a covenant of works, that is, while he is not brought into a state of justification, he is under the dominion of sin; and therefore he is utterly incapable of doing any work which is acceptable to God. According to this delightful passage, a man must not be under the law as a covenant, but under grace; that is, he must be justified freely by the grace of God, in order to the first exercise of that repentance which is spiritually good and acceptable to God.

2. *This notion that the exercise of true repentance is previously necessary to the reception of pardon in justification, detracts from the grace of God as manifested in the offers and promises of the glorious gospel.*

In the gospel, pardon of sin through Christ is freely offered to sinners indiscriminately, and is promised immediately to those who believe. 'Through his name whosoever believeth in him shall receive remission of sins' (*Acts* 10:43). Some have insisted that sinners should not come empty-handed to Christ, but that they should bring something with them, especially the exercise of true repentance, if they would obtain the pardon of sin. But how are they to attain the exercise of true repentance, before the forgiveness of sin? They have no power of themselves to repent sincerely. Surely, while they are viewing themselves as still excluded from the pardoning mercy of God, they have not the smallest ground to expect that he will give them grace to exercise such repentance as will be acceptable to him. From what quarter can they hope for grace to repent, whilst as yet their iniquities are unpardoned, and God is viewed as their enemy?

The gospel teaches needy sinners to come as sinners, to come empty-handed to the market of free grace for the remission of sins and all the other blessings of a free salvation (*Isa.* 55:1; *Rev.* 22:17; *Acts* 16:31). But he is far from coming empty-handed who brings the exercise of true repentance with him. If any say that faith, which he is understood to bring with him, is still something; it must be observed that, in the affair of justification, faith is not considered either as an inherent quality, or as a work, but only as the sinner's receiving the gift of that surety-righteousness, by which he is justified. 'Therefore it is of faith', says our apostle, 'that it might be by grace; to the end the promise might be sure to all the seed' (*Rom.* 4:16). Repentance is in this respect very different. There is no spiritual grace which has more of the nature of giving, than true repentance, for it is a turning of the whole man from the love and practice of sin to the love and practice of holiness. There is nothing, therefore, to which a convinced sinner should be farther from allowing any place, among the means of his justification in the sight of God. The abettors of the opinion in question would do well to consider whether, instead of the covenant of grace, they are not taking up with a sort of covenant of works, the tenor of which is, 'Do this: turn sincerely from all sin to God, though thou canst not turn perfectly, and thou shalt live in his favour.' This scheme is evidently of the same nature as that of the covenant of works; for in both, doing is the previous condition of acceptance with God. The difference between the doing in the one, and the doing in the other, as to the degree of obedience, makes no difference in the nature of the two schemes. The one is manifestly a covenant of works, as well as the other. The learned Samuel Rutherford, accordingly, says,

> We would beware of Mr B.'s order of setting repentance, and works of new obedience, before justification; which is indeed a new covenant of works.

The blessed gospel affords an ample warrant to any sinner of mankind who hears it, to receive the free offer which it makes of pardon in and through Christ, immediately upon hearing and understanding the import of it. But according to the false doctrine in question, no man can have a warrant for doing so, till he is satisfied that he has attained the exercise of true repentance. It is laid down by the apostle Paul, as an established maxim, that 'whatsoever is not of faith is sin' (*Rom.* 14:23), that is, if we do any thing, whilst we doubt in our conscience whether it be agreeable to the will of God or not, it is sin. It is evident from the context that the apostle speaks there of the faith of God's command. Suppose, then, that a convinced sinner believes the pardon of sin to be offered in the gospel to none but the true penitent; and, suppose that he is doubting of himself, whether he be such an one or not; he cannot, in that case, without sin, embrace the offered pardon. To him it is forbidden fruit. Nay, before he so much as attempts to receive it, his conscience must be satisfied that his repentance has all the marks which distinguish a true and evangelical repentance from a false and legal repentance. And as it is impossible for a man to discern any thing spiritually good in himself, previous to his first acts of saving faith, he will never be able, according to the self-righteous opinion in question, to find his way to the offered pardon. But how can this consist with the gospel of Christ, which represents justification and eternal life as gifts of immensely free grace, and declares that whosoever will is welcome to take the water of life freely? (*Rev.* 22:17). In the gospel the sinner is directed, first to attempt the immediate acting of true faith in order to attain the exercise of evangelical repentance, but not to attempt the exercise of this repentance in order to warrant the acting of that faith. Justifying and saving faith is the mean of true repentance, and this repentance is not the mean, but the end of that faith.

If any should try to counter this argument, and say that, whilst I hold faith to be the only mean of receiving pardon, a man's assurance of the reality of his faith is as necessary, in order to his embracing of the gospel-offer, as his assurance of the truth of his repentance, on the scheme in question: I would answer by remarking that there is a vast difference between the priority of the exercise of true repentance to pardon, on that scheme, and the priority of the acting of faith, as the mean of receiving pardon. In the former case, the exercise of true repentance is required as a previous qualification, distinct from the reception of the gospel-offer of pardon; and therefore it must be sinful for a man to attempt embracing this offer, until he be satisfied that he has attained that qualification. But in the latter case, true faith is not a qualification previously required, in order to the embracing of the offer of pardon, but is itself the very act of embracing this offer. It is a receiving of pardon, as it is a receiving of Jesus Christ and his righteousness, exhibited in the gospel-offer. Here, the previous consciousness that we have believed cannot be held necessary, in order to the reception of pardon; unless we would think and speak so absurdly as to say that the consciousness of our having already received a benefit is necessary in order to our act of receiving it.

3. *The first exercise of true repentance is not before justification in the sight of God, because it is not previous to the first acting of justifying faith.*

It will not be necessary to say much in illustrating this argument, as it was explained and confirmed in a preceding chapter.

If the exercise of true repentance be not before that of justifying faith, it is not before the pardon of sin in justification. For faith, and justification in the sight of God, are so immediately and closely connected that no other spiritual grace or holy exercise can be considered as coming between them. But if the exercise of true repentance were, in order of nature, after that of justifying faith, and yet before justification, then the exercise of true repentance would come in between faith and justification. It might then be said, in opposition to the apostle Paul, that a man is justified by repentance rather than by faith, as in that case, repentance would be connected more immediately with justification than with faith. Then it might be affirmed that, as repentance is the nearest mean of justification, it should be regarded as the most important and noble one. For it is highly reasonable to prefer the immediate and nearest mean, before the one which is intermediate and remote. Hence it would come to pass that, in the pardon of sin, the exercise of repentance should be considered as the more noble and important mean. Should a convinced and alarmed sinner say that he attempts to believe, and to rely immediately on Jesus Christ for pardon, this question, according to that self-righteous scheme, must be put to him: Do you repent sincerely of all your sins? Your acting of faith cannot obtain pardon, without the exercise of genuine repentance. Thus, then, the exercise of true repentance, as a mean of attaining the pardon of sin, is preferable to the acting of faith; since without it, faith can do nothing. How absurd is all this, and how far from being the doctrine of the gospel!

Again, the first exercise of evangelical repentance, as it is distinguished from that of justifying faith, comes necessarily in order of nature after it. It is true, as has been remarked already, that the word repentance in Scripture sometimes expresses the whole of that change which takes place in the conversion of a sinner to God. In this sense it includes faith in Jesus Christ. Now it would be improper to say of repentance in this view, that it is after the acting of faith in Christ. Yet it remains true, that the exercise of true repentance taken in a strict sense, as denoting godly sorrow for sin and sincere endeavours after new obedience, is distinct from the acting of justifying faith, and in order of nature follows it. And although, in this sense, repentance is implied in faith, as an effect is implied in its cause, yet it cannot from this be inferred, that the exercise of the former is not, in order of nature, after that of the latter. The fruit of a tree may be said to have always been seminally, or as to its principles, in the tree; yet none, on that account, will hesitate to say that the fruit, as to its natural order, is after the tree.

To pretend that we may exercise true repentance before the first acting of faith in Jesus Christ, is contrary to all those passages of Scripture which assert the necessity of faith in order to our living, standing, or walking, in a spiritual manner; or in order to our performing any other duty in a manner acceptable to God (*Gal.* 2:20; *2 Cor.* 1:24; 5:7; *Heb.* 11:6; *John* 15:4-5). It is true, as already hinted, that repentance is, in some passages, mentioned before faith (*Mark* 1:15; *Acts* 20:21). But things are not mentioned in Scripture, always according to the order of nature. For instance, it is not according to that order that, in 2 Peter 1:10, the calling of believers is put before their election; and that, in the apostolic benediction, 2 Corinthians 13:14, the grace of our Lord Jesus Christ is put before the love of the Father. So in the places in which repentance is mentioned before faith, what is intended is not to show the natural order; but rather, first to propose repentance as the end, and then faith, as the instituted means of compassing that end.

I conclude, then, that as the first exercise of true repentance is after the first acting of faith in Christ, so it is after the pardon of sin in justification, which is received by faith only.

4. *The first exercise of evangelical repentance is not before the pardon of sin in the act of justification, because it is not before the exercise of supreme love to God in Christ.*

That the exercise of true repentance is not prior to the exercise of love to God, but on the contrary, springs from this exercise, appears from the example of the penitent woman, recorded in Luke 7:37-48. Whilst Jesus was sitting at meat in a Pharisee's house, a woman who was a sinner 'stood at his feet behind him weeping, and began to wash his feet with tears, and did wipe them with the hairs of her head, and kissed his feet, and anointed them with the ointment.' Her tears were tears of godly sorrow for her many sins; and our Lord, whose judgment is always according to truth, said that they flowed from love. She loved much; and her tears, as well as the several instances of her singular attention to our Lord at that time, sprang from love to him. The exercise of true repentance, then, proceeds from unfeigned love to God; and so, in order of nature, is posterior to it. Hence is this injunction of the Psalmist, 'Ye that love the Lord hate evil' (*Psa.* 97:10). Hatred of evil, which is a part of evangelical repentance, is a consequence and a sure proof of genuine love to the Lord. No sorrow for sin, nor hatred of it, nor turning from it, belongs to true repentance, but that which proceeds from, and follows, unfeigned love to Christ and to God in him.

Now, while the exercise of true repentance flows from supreme love to God, the exercise of this love proceeds, under the sanctifying influences of the Holy Spirit, from the forgiveness of sins in justification. That it does so is evident from our Lord's parable of the two debtors, in the place already referred to. For, by this parable he shows plainly that, as an effect is still according to its cause so our love to God will be according to the forgiveness of our sins, received by faith. In this sense we are to understand what our Lord said to the Pharisee respecting the woman: 'I say unto thee, her sins, which are many, are forgiven; for she loved much.' The conjunction, *for*, does not always denote the cause of a thing, but sometimes the effect and evidence of it;[2] as when we say, 'The spring is come, for the plants begin to bud.' So the Lord Jesus said to his disciples, 'The Father himself loveth you; for ye have loved me' (*John* 16:27), that is, your love to me is an effect and evidence of the Father's love to you.

Our Lord's meaning in the parable is plainly this: the person who is forgiven most will love most. But that poor woman, and not Simon the Pharisee, loves most. Therefore she is the person who is forgiven most. Her love is a full proof that her sins, how many so ever they have been, are all graciously forgiven. As to the mean or instrument by which this woman received the forgiveness of her sins, our Lord informs us what it was, when he said to her, 'Thy faith hath saved thee,'—thy faith, not thy repentance, nor thy tears. Chemnitius, commenting on the story, says well:

From the fruits of love, our Lord shows that the sins of this woman were forgiven. When he had said, 'Her sins are forgiven; for she loved much', he immediately adds (to prevent the mistake of his meaning, with regard to the order of cause and effect), 'But to whom little is forgiven, the same loveth little.' He declares again and again

---

[2] 'That the woman's love', says Ames, 'is here pointed out as the effect of the pardon of her sins, is evident from the whole discourse.'

that remission of sin goes before, and that love follows. Having said, 'The creditor frankly forgave them both', he adds, 'Which of them will love him most?' Here it is observable, that the expression, *will love him,* is in the future tense; whereas the expression, *he forgave them,* is in the preterite or past tense; intimating that a person's love to God follows the remission of sins, as the future follows the past. Here Christ shows us whence true love to him springs . . . Hence it is, that unless the gospel, which proclaims a free grant of the forgiveness of sins, be received by faith, the true love of God can neither enter into, nor abide in any soul.

Although a man does not begin to exercise true repentance before the pardon of his sins in justification, yet he may begin the exercise of it before he attains a distinct sense of his being already in a justified state. The influence of pardoning mercy, apprehended by faith, will produce true love to God, and the exercise of evangelical repentance, not indeed before the sinner has been justified, but before he has attained a comfortable sense of his justification. Thus the woman's repentance, above mentioned, which followed the forgiveness of her sins, was before the comfortable sense of this forgiveness, arising from justification our Lord's intimation of it (*Luke* 7:48), by saying to her, 'Thy sins are forgiven'; and by adding, 'Thy faith hath saved thee; go in peace.'

Thus it is plain that unfeigned love to God is a fruit of the forgiveness of sin in justification, and therefore follows it; but the first exercise of true repentance flows from that love, and so, in order of nature, is after it.

Therefore the first exercise of true repentance follows the pardon of sin in the act of justification. The former is an inseparable consequence of the latter. Justifying faith works by love, and love produces the exercise of evangelical repentance.

5. Lastly, that the pardon of sin in justification goes before the first exercise of evangelical repentance is most agreeable to the order in which God has promised to bestow these inestimable blessings, upon his people.

His promises of them run thus: 'I have blotted out, as a thick cloud, thy transgressions, and as a cloud thy sins: return unto me; for I have redeemed thee' (*Isa.* 42:22). 'I will establish my covenant with thee; . . . that thou mayest remember and be confounded, and never open thy mouth any more, because of thy shame, when I am pacified toward thee for all that thou hast done, saith the Lord GOD' (*Ezek.* 16:62-63). 'I will sprinkle clean water upon you', that is, the blood of Messiah, for the remission of sins, and 'ye shall be clean', judicially absolved from every charge of guilt (*Ezek.* 36:25).[3] 'A new heart will I give you . . . I will put my spirit within you, and cause you to walk in my statutes, and ye shall keep my judgments and do them' (*Ezek.* 36:26-27). 'Then shall ye remember your own evil ways, and your doings that were not good, and shall loathe yourselves in your own sight, for your

---

[3] It is proper to understand this as a promise of the remission of sin; as being a blessing distinct from regeneration and sanctification promised in the two verses immediately following.

iniquities, and for your abominations' (*Ezek.* 36:31). 'I will heal their backsliding . . . Ephraim shall say, What have I to do any more with idols?' (*Hos.* 14:4, 8). No exercise of repentance is described in these passages, but what follows the forgiveness of sin. This is the native order of these blessings; and none should attempt to disturb or invert it. The argument from these passages is, not only that the state of justification is mentioned before the exercise of true repentance; but that the latter is represented as the native effect of the former. The grace of Jehovah toward Israel, manifested in his being pacified toward them for all that they have done, fills them with penitential shame and self-loathing. Ephraim's resolution to have no more to do with idols is the native consequence or effect of the healing of his backsliding. The consequence of Jehovah's sprinkling of clean water upon them, and making them clean, is that they remember their own evil ways, and their doings that were not good, and loathe themselves in their own sight. That a legal repentance, proceeding from legal convictions and a dread of Divine judgments, goes before justification is readily granted. But that any exercise of evangelical repentance, of that spiritual repentance which the Lord secures to his people in those promises, goes before it, has never been proved.

From these arguments it is evident that, in order of nature, justification in the sight of God, or forgiveness of sin in justification, precedes the first exercise of true repentance. But seeing the principle of evangelical repentance is implanted in the soul before justification, none is justified in the sight of God, but he who, in this sense, is already a true penitent. It is only the habit and the exercise of true repentance that follow the act of justification.

�֎

Is it true, then, that no sinner is pardoned but the penitent sinner, the sinner who has the principle of true repentance already in his heart? It plainly follows that no pardoned sinner can continue impenitent. He has already the root or principle of true repentance; and when he so believes as to be justified by faith, this principle will, under the sanctifying influences of the Holy Spirit, become a habit, and be excited to immediate exercise. Every man who is justified is entitled to sanctification, of which the habit and exercise of true repentance are essential parts. A pardoned sinner, then, cannot but exercise, and advance in the exercise of evangelical repentance.

From what has been said, the candid reader may see the meaning of this assertion of the apostle Paul, '[God] justifieth the ungodly' (*Rom.* 4:5). The meaning cannot be that he justifies an unregenerate sinner. By the ungodly here is not meant the unregenerate, but the regenerate sinner, who has no legal godliness, no righteousness of his own pleadable in law, as a ground of justification in the sight of God. If this were not the meaning, it would follow that justification is before regeneration; contrary to the order mentioned by our apostle (*Rom.* 8:30), and to that in the *Shorter Catechism*. A legal ungodliness is in the regenerate sinner before justification by faith. He sees that he has no godliness, no righteousness of his own to rely on, as a ground of justification. That man is to be deemed ungodly who has no godliness that the omniscient Judge can admit as a ground of title to justification. Because he has not, before the righteousness of Jesus Christ be imputed to him, a perfect righteousness for justification, in the eye of the law he is ungodly, have what he will. If the sentence should pass upon him, on the ground of his principles of holiness, the Judge could not but find him, in the eye of the law, ungodly, and as such condemn him. Besides, God justifies him who hitherto was ungodly. The sense of the words may be the same as when our Lord said, 'The blind see', and 'the deaf hear' (*Luke* 7:22). His meaning cannot be that those persons were actually blind when they saw, or deaf when they heard; but that having been once so, they now saw and heard. In legal reckoning, that man is ungodly who has broken any of the commands of God's law. That the ungodly should be justified by his own righteousness is therefore a contradiction in the eye of the law; as much as if we should say that the same individual has at once broken the law, and perfectly kept it. For if he is in himself ungodly, where are his works of perfect righteousness? This view of the text under consideration is most agreeable to the apostle's design; which is, to guard the doctrine of justification by the free grace of God, against the errors of legal teachers.

Hence also it is manifest that the convinced sinner should attempt to believe that Christ died for the remission of his sins, in order to repent of them. No sinner can, in the exercise of true repentance, return to God, but by Christ the way; and none can return by Christ, otherwise than by believing in him. The convinced sinner, then, should believe or trust that Jesus Christ died to take away his sins, in order to turn from them to God. He should rely on the consummate righteousness of Christ for the pardon of them, in order to hate and forsake them. It is only when he is enabled cordially to trust, that God puts away his iniquities from him, by remission; and that he is inclined and resolved, through grace, to put them away from himself, by evangelical repentance. 'Let them that will', says a godly and judicious writer,

> repent, that Christ may do for them; I shall desire always to believe what Christ hath done for me, that I may repent; not doubting but that the being instructed therein is the plain way to smiting on the thigh, and saying, What have I done?

No sin is truly repented of, till it be pardoned; nor is the sinner ever melted so much into godly sorrow, as when he knows that his iniquities are forgiven. The faith of pardon melts the adamantine heart, makes the head waters, and the eyes a fountain of tears. It is by viewing our sins, by an appropriating faith, as laid upon the Lamb of God, and him as pierced for them, that we attain the lively exercise of evangelical repentance. The more our hearts are enabled to trust that the Lord Jesus 'was wounded for our transgressions, and was bruised for our iniquities' (*Isa.* 53:5), the more will we abhor them, and turn from the love and practice of them.

[167]

From what has been advanced it clearly appears that it is the immediate duty of every sinner who hears the gospel to trust in Christ and his righteousness for justification. When he sincerely attempts this first duty, the exercise of true repentance will necessarily follow. When he believes in the Lord Jesus for justification, at the same time he trusts in him for sanctification, for grace to enable him to repent of all his sins. And according to his faith it is unto him. The design of his justification is not to lay a foundation for his continuance in sin, but that he may 'go and sin no more' (*John* 8:11). It will be absolutely impossible for him to exercise evangelical repentance, till his sins be pardoned; for till they be forgiven, God is a consuming fire to him. The curse of the law abides on him, and intercepts the communication of that grace which is necessary to produce the exercise of true repentance. Was he wont to trust in himself, and in his own works? In order to exercise repentance unto life, his heart must turn to Jesus Christ for a better righteousness, and thereby for eternal life. It must turn from every false ground of hope, and rely only on Christ, looking not to his own penitential tears, nor to his own graces or duties; but 'looking for the mercy of our Lord Jesus Christ unto eternal life' (*Jude* 21).

Let no sinner conclude that his exercise of repentance atones for his crimes, or entitles him in the smallest degree to the favour of God and the felicity of heaven. He must receive by faith the atonement made by the Lord Jesus, and have his sins all forgiven on the ground of it, before he can begin to exercise the least true repentance. He must receive also the gift of righteousness, and in justification be accepted as righteous, and so be entitled to the happiness of heaven, before he can begin the exercise of that repentance which is acceptable to God. How then can his repentance atone for his iniquities, or entitle him to the favour of God and to the happiness of heaven? How can that evangelical repentance, which he is incapable of exercising till after his sins be all forgiven on the ground of an infinite atonement imputed to him, make atonement for them? How can that true repentance, which he cannot exercise until in justification he be already entitled to eternal life, entitle him to eternal life? Does not the consummate righteousness of Jesus Christ, imputed for justification, entitle the believer fully to it? What need is there, then, that his repentance should entitle him? How can that exercise of repentance which is the consequence of pardon, afford a previous title to pardon? or that which is a part of eternal life be a ground of right to eternal life? As to that legal repentance which an alarmed sinner is supposed to exercise before faith and justification, and which is an abomination to the Lord—how can that which is itself sin, satisfy Divine justice for sin? How is it possible that that which merits eternal death, should at the same time merit for the sinner eternal life? How can that proud, that pharisaical penitence, on which the sinner depends for pardon of sin and a right to life, procure for him either the one or the other? O sinner, believe and repent, and that without delay; but do not in the least depend on your exercise of them, either for pardon of sin, or for a title to the smallest blessing from the Lord. Your immediate duty is, by the acting of faith, to receive Christ as Jehovah your Righteousness for justification, and to receive from his fullness that evangelical repentance which is included in sanctification. So shall you repent in such a manner as will please God.

From what has been said it is plain that the exercise of true repentance is necessary, in order to a believer's attaining the comfortable sense of pardon in justification. It is an evidence of his having received judicial pardon and so, is a mean of his attaining the assurance that he is already in a state of pardon. Although the exercise of true repentance is not requisite to the obtaining judicial remission, seeing faith alone is the instrument of receiving this, yet it is necessary if a man is to attain the assurance of gospel blessings. It usually precedes a satisfying sense of judicial pardon. It was not till after the woman who washed our Lord's feet with tears, and wiped them with the hairs of her head, had thereby expressed that love and penitence which were the consequences of the pardon of her sins, that he intimated her pardon to her. He said to her, after her sins had been forgiven, and after she had exercised that repentance which was the evidence of her state of pardon, 'Thy sins are forgiven; . . . thy faith hath saved thee; go in peace' (*Luke* 7:48, 50). Would you then, believer, who are oppressed with doubts and fears respecting the remission of your sins, attain joyful intimations that they are all forgiven? O renew, and frequently renew, not only the acting of humble confidence in your adorable Redeemer for all his salvation, but also the exercise of evangelical repentance. Godly sorrow is sweet, is delicious sorrow. It is often attended by a delightful sense of redeeming love and of justifying grace. Whilst, with tears of sorrow and of gratitude, you praise a forgiving God and a bleeding Saviour, you realize this paradox: 'sorrowful, yet always rejoicing' (2 *Cor.* 6:10). Your melting seasons of penitential sorrow will usually pave the way for your strongest and sweetest consolations.

It is manifest also from what has been argued, that when the Lord inflicts upon believers fatherly chastisement for their sins against him, it is not commonly removed, till they renew, with deep concern, the exercise of faith and repentance. The exercise of true repentance, as well as of faith, is necessary to the believer's attainment of fatherly pardon, or of deliverance from the painful effects of his having provoked the anger of his heavenly Father. The reason of this is plain. The Lord's design in inflicting paternal strokes is that he may correct his disobedient child, or lead him to spiritual, evangelical, and deep repentance. When, therefore, the Lord has inflicted fatherly strokes upon the believer for his offences, he will not remove them until, by the exercise of faith and repentance, the Christian amends his ways and his doings (*Jer.* 7:3), and so answers his gracious design in inflicting them (*Isa.* 27:9). When one sort prevails not, the Lord inflicts another, and perhaps a third, until, in the hand of his Holy Spirit, they become effectual. Not that the sin, upon the exercise of repentance, is immediately pardoned, and the chastisement removed. For the Lord, by inflicting paternal chastisements, has other designs to accomplish besides the repentance of the believer. For example, he intends that his injured honour should be vindicated, and that others may see and fear and do no more wickedly. Believer, is it your desire to be in any degree exempted from the painful infliction of paternal chastisements? Be always on your guard, then, against the commission of any known sin, and the omission, even for once, of any known duty. Exercise frequently faith and repentance. Study to perform every duty, as well as to exercise every grace, with increasing spirituality. Thus you will 'walk worthy of the Lord unto all pleasing' (*Col.* 1:10).

In conclusion: It may justly be inferred from what has been stated that faith and repentance are parts, as well as means of salvation. Faith, in one view of it, is the mean or instrument of vital union with Christ, and of communion with him, in his righteousness and salvation. True repentance also, in one view, is an instituted mean of attaining the perfection of salvation; or rather, it is our walking in the way to the perfection of it. Faith and repentance, then, are doubtless to be urged on the hearers of the gospel, as internal means of salvation. They are to be inculcated on believers as the means of advancing in holiness, and of attaining in due time to the perfection of holiness and happiness. In this view, the frequent exercise of them is required in the law. The more the true Christian uses these internal means of salvation, and the less he depends on his use of them, the more speedily will he advance toward perfection.

True faith and repentance, in another point of view, are essential parts of salvation. In the gospel they are both promised as parts of eternal life or salvation. They are spiritual graces, implanted in the soul of an elect sinner at regeneration; and so they are parts of salvation in its commencement and progress in the soul. The more a believer makes progress in the habit and exercise of faith and repentance, the more does he advance in salvation from the power and practice of all sin. These spiritual graces are parts of salvation, or they are parts of true holiness, which is eternal life begun and advancing in the soul. Holiness is the happiness of the rational creature. To conceive of happiness without it would be a contradiction, seeing it is the main ingredient in all true happiness. To bring sinners to holiness, therefore, was, in subordination to the glory of God, the great design of Christ's undertaking.

To press holiness upon sinners, merely as the mean or way of attaining happiness, will lead them blindly to imagine that happiness is something distinct from holiness, and is to be procured by it. If holiness which includes faith and repentance be urged upon sinners, merely as the way or mean of attaining salvation, and never as the leading part of salvation, nor as the end to be aimed at, it will have a native tendency to put them upon doing for life, and not doing from life. It will encourage them to seek and to expect salvation according to a covenant of works, or to depend on their supposed faith, repentance, and holiness, as grounds of title to future happiness. Surely, there can be no impropriety or absurdity, in considering the same thing as a mean in one respect, and as an end in another. Holiness in this world is a mean of attaining to the perfection of it in heaven, as the end; and in this view it is distinct from the end. But then it is no less clear that it is not of a different nature from the perfect holiness or happiness of the saints in heaven, but is different from it only in degree. It is, therefore, in itself to be regarded as an end which every sinner ought to compass by appointed means, especially by the diligent exercise of faith and repentance.

8: OBJECTIONS ANSWERED

Various objections have been keenly urged against the teaching that faith, and the pardon of sin in justification, precede the first exercise of true repentance. I shall here endeavour to return answers to such of them as are the most plausible.

1. It has been objected, 'that there are several passages of Scripture, such as Luke 3:3 and 24:47 and Acts 5:31, in which repentance is mentioned before the forgiveness of sins.'

With regard to these and similar passages, it may be proper to recollect what has been said already concerning the mention of repentance before faith; namely, that the order in which things are mentioned in Scripture is not, in every instance, the order of nature. Repentance or a turning from sin to God, being a duty required by the dictates even of a natural conscience, may well be first preached to sinners, in order to convince them at once of the necessity of it, and of their natural inability to exercise it; and then will properly follow the doctrine and offer of the forgiveness of sins, the faith of which is the principal mean of attaining the exercise of that repentance. In this view, repentance might be preached by John the Baptist and the apostles of Christ, before the doctrine of forgiveness. Besides, the word repentance, appears to be sometimes used to express the relinquishing of wrong opinions. Accordingly, when John exhorted the Jews to repent, he may be understood as inviting them to relinquish the error of the Pharisees about a temporal Messiah, and about justification in the sight of God by the works of the law; and that of the Sadducees concerning the resurrection. When Peter told them that they had crucified him whom God now glorified, he showed them how they came to commit that most atrocious crime. 'Through ignorance ye did it, as did also your rulers' (*Acts* 3:17). He then corrects their mistake, informing them that, according to the prophecies respecting Messiah, he was to suffer the very things which they had inflicted upon Jesus of Nazareth (verse 18). Hence he urges them to change their mind, to relinquish the destructive error with respect to Messiah into which they had fallen, and to turn to the Lord by embracing his gospel (verse 19). One reason for not understanding the word *repent* here to mean evangelical repentance, is that this repentance is evidently included in the next phrase, 'be converted'. But were it granted that the term repent here might signify evangelical repentance, yet this passage would not prove such repentance to be prior to the forgiveness of sins in justification. For 'the blotting out of sins' here may signify, not the formal pardon of them in the act of justification, but the manifestation of that pardon. For in Scripture a thing is often said to be done, when it is manifested. By 'the times of refreshing from the presence of the Lord', Calvin, Beza, Piscator, Aretius, and other judicious commentators, understand the day of judgment, when the saints shall be refreshed by the most public and honourable declaration of their state of pardon (verses 20-21). For the time here referred to is 'the time of restitution of all things', when Christ shall be sent from heaven to judge the world. Now the apostle's teaching, that repentance is before the glorious declaration of pardon at the last day, is surely no proof that the exercise of true repentance goes before the act of pardon itself. In a word, repentance is sometimes put for the whole of conversion to God, including both faith and turning from sin to him. This seems to be the meaning of it in the words, 'Then hath God also to the Gentiles granted repentance unto life' (Acts 11:18). Repentance in this its large acceptation may be said to be both before and after the pardon of sin in justification; before it, in respect of faith receiving Christ as 'Jehovah our Righteousness', and after it, in respect of godly sorrow for sin and turning from it to God.

As to the expression in Luke 3:3, 'John first declares', says Calvin on the place,

> that the kingdom of heaven is at hand; and having thus proposed the grace of God to his hearers, he thence exhorts them to repent. Hence it appears that the mercy

of God, by which he restores the lost, is the ground upon which repentance proceeds. In this sense, Mark and Luke say that John preached the baptism of repentance for the remission of sins; not to intimate, as some ignorantly suppose, that repentance is the cause of the remission of sins; but to teach us that, as the free love of God is first in embracing poor sinners, not imputing their sins unto them, so this pardon of sins is granted us in Christ; not that God may indulge us in our sins, but that he may heal us and deliver us from them.' Piscator on the same place says, 'The baptism of repentance means that this ordinance was used to testify and profess repentance. The words, *for the remission of sins*, depend immediately, not on the word preached, nor on the word repentance, but on the word baptism; and the import of the exhortation is, that baptism serves to signify and seal the remission of sins.

2. *Some have objected to the doctrine above stated, 'that in Acts 2:38 and 8:22, the exhortations to the exercise of repentance are prefixed to the attaining of pardon, intimating that, if sinners do not repent, they have no ground to expect the remission of their sins. The exercise of true repentance, therefore, must precede the pardon of sin in justification.'*

In answer to this, let it be observed that in those passages, the whole way of a sinner's returning to God is in general proposed. On this position, Calvin expresses himself thus, 'Truly I am not ignorant that, under the name of repentance, is comprehended the whole turning to God, whereof faith is not the least part!'[1] If, before a sinner

[1] *Institutes*, 3:3:5.

can be pardoned, it is requisite that he exercise faith and repentance and walk in good works, then repentance and good works are made equal with faith as the means of justification; for it is clear that obedience rendered by the regenerate man is comprehended in the whole import of returning to God. Now unless our whole turning to God more generally be an instituted mean of our attaining the remission of sins, the passages alleged prove nothing to the purpose. As to the first of them, 'Repent and be baptized . . . for the remission of sins' (*Acts* 2:38), who does not see that the command to be baptized is prefixed to the remission of sins, as well as the command to repent? Must it then follow that baptism is a necessary mean in order to attain the remission of sins? The argument is of as much force for baptism as it is for repentance. Mention is indeed made of remission, but not by way of promise. Nay, nothing is said here of a formal reception of remission. For, as Piscator well observes, 'These words, *for the remission of sins,* do not depend on the word *repent,* but on the words *be baptized.*' The meaning, then, of the apostle's exhortation to those convinced sinners, is that they should repent, that is, should turn to God in Christ by faith and repentance; and that they should receive baptism, not as a mean of obtaining the remission of sins, but as a testimony of their receiving that, and every other spiritual blessing in Christ, by means of faith in him. It is manifest, from the connection denoted by the causal particle *for,* in verse 39, that the apostle there exhibits the promise of pardon and salvation as the ground upon which he calls them to repent; as if he had said, 'I exhort you to repent; and in order that you may do so in a spiritual and acceptable manner, believe that the promise is to you. You are pricked in your heart, but do not despond; for the promise of the Spirit, and of a free salvation, is graciously directed in offer to you. Therefore turn wholly to God, by faith, repentance, and new obedience; and for assurance of the remission of your sins, receive baptism as the sign and seal of the covenant.'

As to the last passage alleged (*Acts* 8:22), it is plain that the apostle prefixes the command to pray, to what he says of forgiveness, as well as the command to repent; yet surely it cannot hence be concluded, that acceptable prayer goes before the forgiveness of sin in justification. But here, as before, repentance is put for the whole way of turning to the Lord.

3. *Some have argued for the priority of the exercise of true repentance to the pardon of sin in justification, from these words of our Lord to Saul of Tarsus, 'I send thee to open their eyes, and to turn them from darkness to light, and from the power of Satan unto God, that they may receive forgiveness of sins, and inheritance among them which are sanctified by faith that is in me' (Acts 26:18).*

In answer, let it be observed that here our blessed Lord first shows how he works faith in the hearts of sinners by means of the gospel: namely, by opening their eyes, and turning them from darkness to light, and from the power of Satan unto God. He next declares that, by means of faith thus wrought, they receive forgiveness of sins, and inheritance among them who are sanctified by faith that is in him. It is urged that this clause, 'to turn them from the power of Satan unto God', may signify the exercise of true repentance. I answer, that as these words, 'to turn them from darkness to light, and from the power of Satan unto God,' plainly describe the work of the Spirit of Christ by means of the gospel, they are to be understood of regeneration, which is attributed to the gospel as a mean of it (*James* 1:18; *1 Pet.* 1:23). The turning here mentioned is the work of the Spirit of Christ, in which sinners are passive. The first expression, 'to open their eyes', is used to describe the work of Christ (*Isa.* 43:7); but it is nowhere said to be the sinner's act. The next phrase, 'to turn them from darkness to light, and from the power of Satan unto God', is of the same meaning with bringing out the prisoners from the prison, and them that sit in darkness out of the prison-house; a work which, in the same passage, is also ascribed to Christ, but nowhere in Scripture to the sinner himself.

Hence the expressions in question cannot be understood of the exercise of true repentance; for this is the exercise or work of a regenerate sinner. But the following expression, 'that they may receive', may be connected with these words at the end of the verse, 'by faith that is in me'; and may well be understood of the sinner's act of receiving forgiveness and the inheritance of eternal life by faith, which is necessarily followed by the exercise of evangelical repentance. Thus the words of the Lord Jesus in this passage represent a sinner's receiving by faith the forgiveness of sins, and not the exercise of true repentance, as the first or most immediate effect of regeneration; and so, they serve much to confirm the priority of pardon to the first exercise of that repentance. If the expression, 'by faith that is in me', be understood to be immediately connected with the word 'sanctified', it will be a further confirmation of the same doctrine. For thus the faith, which receives forgiveness of sins, is declared to be the means of sanctification. But if that faith be the means of sanctification, it is of course the means of attaining the exercise of true repentance; for this repentance, as has been already stated, is included in sanctification. The first act of justifying and saving faith, therefore, is before the first exercise of true repentance, as the means are, in order of nature, prior to the end.

4. *Some have maintained 'that the following texts prove the first exercise of evangelical repentance to be prior to the forgiveness of sins in justification: Luke 13:3, 5; Prov. 28:13; Jer. 4:1, 3-4; Ezek. 33:11; and Isa. 55:7.'*

To this it may be answered, that the passage in Luke 13:3, 5 does not hold forth a connection between repentance and forgiveness, but merely between impenitence and perishing. The difference between these two connections is great. Let the argument be this: Except ye repent, ye shall perish. Therefore if ye do repent, ye shall live. Here, as Thomas Boston well observes, 'The consequent is true, but the consequence is naught.' It is no better reasoning than it would be to say, Our evil works will damn us, therefore our good works will save us; or, as if we should say, if we do not pray, we shall perish; therefore if we do pray, we shall live. When the Papists argued that men must be justified by their good works, because they are condemned for the want of them, Calvin's answer to them was to this purpose: The contraries here are not equal; for one deviation, however, small, from the perfect rule of God's law, renders a person unrighteous, and liable to eternal death (*James* 1:20). But it is not one or a few good works, but an unremitted course of obedience, without the smallest defect, that will constitute a person righteous in the sight of God. And it is a maxim, with respect to a particular action, that it is not morally good unless it have all the requisites of a good work. The want but of one of them renders it evil. In like manner, not repenting simply or of itself, is sufficient to make us perish; but who will say that repentance of itself is, even in the way of means, sufficient to save us? There is indeed no salvation without repentance. But if every thing without which men shall perish must go before a state of justification, as a mean of attaining to it, then a holy life, and perseverance in it until death, must go before justification; and then it will follow, that justification in the sight of God is not to be attained before death. For the Scriptures plainly declare, that without holiness and enduring to the end, as well as without repentance, men shall undoubtedly perish (*Heb.* 10:39; 12:14). They also declare, 'That all who believe, are justified from all things,' and that to them there is no condemnation (*Acts* 13:39; *Rom.* 8:1).

Here we learn that, as soon as a sinner begins cordially to believe in him who is Jehovah our Righteousness, his justification before God is, at that instant, complete and irrevocable.

As to Proverbs 28:13, it serves clearly to teach us that none evidences himself to be a sharer in the pardoning mercy of God in Christ, but he who sincerely confesses and forsakes his sins. To affirm that he whom the Holy Spirit brings to this exercise shall have mercy during the after course of his life (*Psa.* 23:6), and at the day of judgment (2 *Tim.* 1:18), is perfectly consistent with asserting that the mercy of a state of pardon is, in order of nature, prior to that exercise. Samuel Rutherford commenting on the passage, observes that the Holy Ghost is not here speaking about order, as if penitent confession, and forsaking of all sin, must go before forgiveness; but the Lord designs the persons pardoned, that they must be such as forsake their sins (*Prov.* 28:13). There is much reason for this; because many who cover their sins, and do not forsake them, will yet pretend to share in pardoning mercy. Such have much need to be undeceived. Besides, it should be observed that the expression in this text may include the confession of open and scandalous sins before men, and their exercise of mercy toward such sinners; and it may also include the practice of good works in general, as is evident from the import of forsaking sin (*Matt.* 5:7; *Prov.* 14:21). Now, will any Protestant deliberately say that the practice of good works in general is the previous condition of justification in the sight of God?

With respect to Jeremiah 4:1, 3-4 and Ezekiel 33:11, it may be remarked, that, in these texts repentance is either taken in its large sense, for the whole of conversion, in which faith in Jesus Christ, and receiving the remission of sins, as well as repentance strictly taken, is comprehended; or the duty is simply required; while the right manner of performing it, and the connection of it with privileges and with other duties, are to be learned by comparing other passages of Scripture on the same subject. Such commands are given to persons, both before justification, for conviction, and after it, for direction, with declarations of a certain connection between true repentance and life, and that in perfect consistency with the priority of pardon in justification to the exercise of such repentance. No texts of Scripture have ever been or can be produced, which teach that God has either brought sinners to the exercise of evangelical repentance, or has promised to do so, before the faith of his pardoning mercy.

As to Isaiah 55:11, it is evidently the design of this remarkable passage to set before the sinner the pardoning mercy of God in Christ that he may first believe or trust in it for pardon, and for grace to return to God; and then, that by this faith or trust, he may begin the exercise of true repentance, in turning from his wicked way and thoughts. 'Here', says Calvin upon the text,

> the context is to be carefully attended to: for the prophet shows that men must have the previous faith or confidence of pardon, otherwise they cannot be brought unto the exercise of repentance. The doctrine of the Popish

doctors on the nature of repentance is indeed egregious trifling. But even though they were to teach the true nature of it, it would still be unprofitable, while they omit what is the foundation of all right exercise of repentance, the doctrine of free forgiveness of sin, by which alone true peace of conscience can ever be attained. And, indeed, while the sinner is a stranger to this peace of conscience, and views God only as a Judge dragging him to his tribunal to give an account of his ill-spent life, he will flee from God, instead of returning to him, with godly fear and filial obedience.

As the exercise of true repentance is the end, and faith the means of attaining this end, so the sinner is first called to forsake his evil way and his thoughts, and return unto the Lord; and then the absolute promise of pardoning mercy is set before him, that, by applying and trusting it, he may return to the Lord in a spiritual and acceptable manner.

5. *The following objection has been urged against our doctrine: 'God declares to the Israelites that after they should become truly penitent, then he would forgive them: "If they shall confess their iniquity, and the iniquity of their fathers: . . . if their uncircumcised hearts be humbled, and they then accept of the punishment of their iniquity: then will I remember my covenant with Jacob"'* (*Lev.* 26:41-42).

In Ezekiel 3:25, 33, God declares concerning the Jews in Babylon, that he will first bring them to repentance, and then restore them to their land. Solomon, in his prayer at the dedication of the temple, expressly and repeatedly holds forth this doctrine, that repentance is before forgiveness. The temple was a type of the Son of God incarnate. And in all their prayers the penitent Jews looked toward the holy temple, and then God heard in heaven his dwelling place.

> When heaven is shut up, and there is no rain, because they have sinned against thee; if they pray toward this place, and confess thy name, and turn from their sin, *etc*. then hear thou in heaven, and forgive the sin of thy servants (*1 Kings* 8:35-36).

Answer: It cannot be proved that the forgiveness mentioned in these passages is necessarily to be understood of that pardon which is included in the act of justification, and consequently, that all the exercise which is prior to this forgiveness must be before the first acting of faith. For the exercises which preceded this forgiveness, such as prayer and confession of sin, evidently implied the true faith of those who were sincerely engaged in them. To look toward God's holy temple may well be regarded as an Old Testament phrase expressive of believing in God's Holy One. Therefore, as they whose exercise is described in those passages had faith in Messiah before the forgiveness there mentioned, it follows that they were in a state of justification before that exercise. Forgiveness of sin, as has been observed already, sometimes signifies the manifestation of God's favour toward his people, in the removal of temporal calamities from them. In this sense I am led to understand forgiveness in the passages under consideration, and particularly in the deliverance of the Jewish church from her captivity. If it be granted that true believers in that church were, by the sentence of justification before God, already exempted from eternal wrath, it will not follow that the forgiveness there mentioned is to be understood of this justifying sentence, and not of the removal of temporal calamities. For the deliverance of believers from temporal strokes, the effects of paternal anger, doubtless may be, and often is, a token to them, of the sentence of their justification, which may have taken place long before. 'It is clear', says Thomas Boston,

> that in such passages, the people are considered in their national capacity, under national strokes for national sins, for the removal of which, repentance of the same kind is required. And though, in such a general repentance of a people, they who believe are spiritually and theologically serious, and with a removal of the common calamity from the society of which they are members, get God's countenance to shine on their souls; yet the generality are never evangelically penitent. But moral seriousness in such a case, according to the Lord's dealing with nations, is a mean of getting these temporal strokes removed, as may be seen in the case of the Ninevites, and many times in the case of the Jews. It is generally allowed that there is a twofold being under the covenant of grace, the one external, the other internal. The same person may be under the covenant of works and the covenant of grace; under the former in respect of his soul's state, with God's curse upon him; under the latter, as externally partaking of the external privileges, protections, deliverances, &c. given to the visible church.

Thus God might be said to remember his covenant for the afflicted Israelites, when they as a nation humbled themselves and confessed their sins, and at the same time he might deliver them from the temporal judgments under which they had lain. It is usually upon national repentance that national calamities are removed. But this does not at all concern the point in hand, the question being of the means previously necessary to the pardon of sin, in the act of justification before God; between which, and the subsequent repeated forgivenesses, as has been stated above, there is a vast difference.

6. *It has been urged 'that, in token of repentance as what must precede forgiveness, the High Priest under the law was, on the great day of atonement, to lay both his hands on the head of a live goat, and confess over him all the iniquities of the children of Israel, and all their transgressions, in all their sins, and thus put them upon the head of the goat, to be sent away into the wilderness. As this was to be done on that solemn occasion, in relation to the iniquities of the children of Israel in general; so, if any particular man at any time committed a sin, he was to bring his bullock, and, in token of confession and repentance, to lay his hand upon its head, and substitute it to die in his room. And if he had not only sinned against God, but in his sin injured his neighbour, he must first, as became a true penitent, make restitution before the sacrifice was offered.'*

A short answer to this must suffice. The act of the

Israelites in the cases now mentioned, in laying their hands on the head of the devoted sacrifice, was a profession of their faith in Messiah as the true antitypical sacrifice, and was a token that they trusted in him for the remission of all their sins. In consequence of that act, supposing it to have been unfeigned, they were actually in a state of pardon, as all true believers are; and therefore, as that act was before the public confession of their sins, so it evidenced their state of pardon to have been before that confession, before that restitution, and the other tokens of their repentance. This, then, is an additional proof of the priority of pardon in justification to the first exercise of true repentance. And that which followed the confession of iniquities in the offering of the sacrifice, namely, the sprinkling of the blood and the sending away of the live goat, corresponded to those comfortable intimations of pardon which the blessed Spirit affords to believers in and after their exercise of evangelical repentance, by means of gospel ordinances.

7. *That which is chiefly urged against the priority of justification by faith to the first exercise of true repentance, is 'the supposed tendency of it to derogate from the necessity and importance of such repentance.'*

This is the old hackneyed objection which has always been urged by legal teachers against the doctrine of a sinner's justification by faith alone; and the solid answers which were given by the apostle Paul to the Judaizing teachers, and by our Reformers to the Papists, in that case, are abundantly sufficient in this. They include the following points:

When we receive the righteousness of Jesus Christ as the ground of our justification, we receive it also as the meritorious and procuring cause of true repentance. The Holy Spirit works repentance in us at the same time in which he works that faith by which we receive the righteousness of Christ for our justification. So that, though justification is before repentance, in order of nature, yet the one cannot be said, at least in the case of adults, to be before the other, in order of time. A believer cannot have the comfortable sense or evidence of his state of pardon without the exercise of true repentance. The negligence of believers in not exercising repentance for particular sins particularly, will bring upon them most heavy corrections in the present life. All who live and die without repentance, shall inevitably perish. It is not a true repentance, or a godly sorrow for sin, to which the pardoning mercy of God and the redeeming love of Christ, apprehended by faith, are not constraining motives.

8. *Once more, it has been said that 'if the necessity of repentance in order to forgiveness, be given up, we shall not be in the practice of urging it on the unconverted. We shall imagine that it will be leading souls astray, to press it before, and in order to believing; and afterward it will be thought unnecessary, as all that is wanted will come of itself.'*

To this ignorant, perverse, and malicious cavil, a short answer must suffice. The objector seems to insinuate that he does not know how sinners can be urged to repentance, and to works worthy of repentance, without representing them as necessary in order to justification. But might not sinners be urged to consider seriously that, while they continue impenitent and unholy, they evidence themselves to be in a state of condemnation, and in the broad way that leads to destruction? Might not they be warned, and pressed to consider, that impenitence obstinately persisted in, will terminate in everlasting destruction? Might not the necessity of true repentance be pressed upon sinners as a motive to their believing in Christ, because such repentance cannot be attained otherwise than by believing in him? Nay, is not this the only suitable and profitable way of urging sinners to evangelical repentance? Is it not as preposterous and unreasonable to press upon poor sinners the necessity of repentance, without pointing out to them the only means by which the exercise of it may be attained, as it would be to say much to a sick man, in order to persuade him to cure himself, whilst he neither himself knows, nor is informed by any other, by what means he may be cured? Has not this unskilful way of urging sinners to the exercise of repentance the most destructive tendency? Does it not lead them to take up with a sort of legal repentance, which fills them with a pharisaical pride, and with such conceit of self-righteousness, as, more than all the gross irregularities of which they pretend to have repented, hardens them in their enmity and opposition to the doctrine of grace?

With respect to true believers, our denying that the first

exercise of evangelical repentance precedes justification, is far from rendering it unnecessary to urge even them, to the daily exercise of this repentance. Although believers have in them the principle and habit of true repentance, and of all other spiritual graces, yet they need, by the admonitions and exhortations of the Word, to be frequently stirred up to the exercise of them. These are necessary, especially in the case of true repentance, because of the deceitful and powerful workings of indwelling sin, and on account of that spiritual sluggishness which is a part of remaining depravity, and which calls for frequent reproof and correction. Hence the exercise of spiritual graces, and the fruits meet for repentance, are commonly as little to be expected even from believers, without the use of means, both internal and external, as the production of a good crop, even in the most fruitful soil, without due cultivation. Accordingly, it appears to be the main design of a great part of Scripture, to excite believers to the lively and daily exercise of evangelical repentance. They are sometimes represented, as wise virgins who slumber and sleep with the foolish, and as having left their first love; and, therefore, they are exhorted to remember from whence they are fallen, and to repent, and do the first works.[2]

---

[2] For most of the arguments in the immediately preceding chapter, and the answers to objections in this, I gladly acknowledge myself indebted to Thomas Boston's *Miscellaneous Questions*, and also to an accurate and able vindication of some points of gospel doctrine, entitled *Precious Truth*, by the Rev. John Anderson of North America. I have freely availed myself of these two excellent publications. They are far from being so well known as they deserve to be.

What has now been advanced constrains me to exhort my reader to mortify, through the Spirit, his unbelief, legal temper, and enmity to God and to the method of salvation by Jesus Christ. These are the principal sources of all the objections that have ever been raised against the truth that the exercise of true repentance comes after faith and justification. O my dear reader! look unto the Lord Jesus Christ, and be you saved from those, and all the other, inveterate corruptions of your nature. Look to him for that supernatural faith of the law, as a violated covenant of works, which issues in deep and thorough conviction of the sin of your nature and life, and especially of the exceeding sinfulness of your unbelief. Look to him also for that saving faith of the glorious gospel, which is a cordial belief of the offers, invitations, and absolute promises of it, with particular application of them; which is the confidence of the heart in him, for all his salvation to yourself in particular; which is a renunciation of your own righteousness, in the affair of justification, and a reliance only on his; and which works by love to God, to Christ, to the Holy Spirit, to the honour of the law, and the glory of the gospel, and to the absolute freeness of Christ's great salvation. By means of the frequent exercise: of this holy faith, you will receive the sanctifying Spirit of Christ, to mortify your legal temper and your natural enmity to the absolute freeness of Christ's salvation. And in proportion as these are mortified, you will cease from objecting against true repentance as a part of that salvation, which Jesus Christ merited for his elect by fulfilling all righteousness for them. You will no longer be disposed to argue against faith, and justification by faith, as previous in order of nature to the first exercise of evangelical repentance. On the contrary, you will spiritually discern, approve, admire, and love the comely order of these, as unalterably fixed by infinite wisdom and love, in the counsel of peace and covenant of grace.

It may be, you have begun already to 'believe to the saving of the soul'; and yet, you are disposed to object against the priority of faith, and of justification, to the first exercise of true repentance. If this be the present frame of your mind, study through grace, I entreat you, to attain more spiritual, clear, and correct views of the truth as it is in Jesus, and to advance quickly in the exercise of spiritual understanding, faith, and love. The more you know, believe, and love the truth, the sooner, will you detect your errors, and with holy abhorrence relinquish them; and the more will you receive the love of the truth, and of the due order of all its parts. The more will you love, not only every particular doctrine or blessing of the glorious gospel, but, the peculiar plan of each in the covenant of grace.

In conclusion: If any of my readers has not yet repented of his innumerable and aggravated sins, I must, before I take my leave of him, again exhort and beseech him to repent without delay. The great and terrible God commands you, in the most peremptory manner, to repent of all your transgressions of his holy law. He 'now commandeth all men everywhere to repent; because he hath appointed a day, in the which he will judge the world in righteousness by that man whom he hath ordained; whereof he hath given assurance unto all men, in that he hath raised him from the dead' (*Acts* 17:30-31). Here the apostle Paul declares that God commands all men to repent. And the powerful motive by which he enforces obedience to the Divine command is this: God 'hath appointed a day in which he will judge the world in righteousness by that man whom he hath ordained'. Believe then, and consider the certainty of that great and terrible day. By raising Christ from the dead, God has given assurance of that day to all men; and therefore, if any man still doubts of the judgment to come, it will be at his peril. The God of truth has not only said, but sworn, that there shall be a day of judgment. 'We shall all stand before the judgment-seat of Christ. For it is written, As I live, saith the Lord, every knee shall bow to me, and every tongue shall confess to God' (*Rom.* 14:10-11). At that awful day, the Lord Jesus will come in the clouds of heaven, with power and great glory, in the glory of his Father, and with his holy angels. At his coming, as the Judge of quick and dead, all the sons and daughters of Adam shall, by the sound of the last trumpet, be summoned to appear before his tribunal. The sound of this trumpet will be so loud, as not only to be heard at once in all places of the earth and all depths of the sea, but to awake all who sleep in the dust, and raise them from death. Then the righteous and omniscient Judge, 'shall sit on the throne of his glory', his 'great white throne' (*Rev.* 20:11), that throne which, as Daniel says, will be 'like the fiery flame' (*Dan.* 7:9). His throne of judgment shall not only be a great, but a white and a fiery throne, white as the snow, and fiery as the flame; white, because no judgment shall proceed from it, but what will be most pure and impartial; and fiery, for it will be inexpressibly terrible to everyone who lives and dies impenitent.

Reflect seriously, O impenitent sinner, that after your hardness and impenitent heart, you are treasuring up to yourself wrath against the day of wrath and revelation of the righteous judgment of God. Oh! if death surprise you in your impenitence the righteous Judge in that day will, with terrible majesty, and the most appalling frown, pronounce on you and all the impenitent this tremendous sentence: 'Depart from me, ye cursed, into everlasting fire, prepared for the devil and his angels' (*Matt.* 25:41). Dreadful doom! To be sentenced to dwell in fire—in fire prepared for the devil and his angels—in everlasting fire, how horrible, how amazing! To be damned by him who came to save sinners from sin and hell, must be double damnation. But thus it shall be. The Lamb of God shall, in that awful day, roar as a lion against you, and by an irreversible sentence from the throne, adjudge you to the most exquisite, the most direful torment, and to the society of devils for ever and ever. No sooner shall the sentence be passed, than it shall be executed: 'These shall go away into everlasting punishment' (*Matt.* 25:46). 'Knowing therefore the terror of the Lord' (2 *Cor.* 5:11), I earnestly entreat you to return by true repentance to the God of all grace.

O be persuaded, while it is called today, to repent and turn from all your transgressions; so iniquity shall not be your ruin. 'As I live, saith the Lord GOD, I have no pleasure in the death of the wicked; but that the wicked turn from his way and live: turn ye, turn ye from your evil ways; for why will ye die' (*Ezek.* 33:11). 'Therefore also now, saith the LORD, turn ye even to me with all your heart, and with fasting, and with weeping, and with mourning; and rend your heart, and not your garments, and turn unto the Lord your God; for he is gracious and merciful, slow to anger, and of great kindness, and repenteth him of the evil' (*Joel* 2:12-13). O comply with these compassionate, and tender invitations! And if you would return to the Lord by true repentance, believe in order to repent. Believe, with application to yourself, the commands and curses of the law as a violated covenant of works, in order to obtain true conviction of your sin and misery. And then believe with particular application the declarations, offers, and promises of the blessed gospel; in order to obtain such a faith-view of the mercy of God in Christ, as will dispose and encourage you to exercise that evangelical repentance which will be acceptable to him. Trust in the Redeemer, that exalted Prince and Saviour, for repentance unto life; and pray in his name to the God of all grace for 'the Spirit of grace and of supplications', to enable you to look upon him whom you have pierced, and to mourn for him.